CAMBRIDGE
UNIVERSITY PRESS

Chemistry
for Cambridge IGCSE™

WORKBOOK

Richard Harwood, Ian Lodge & Mike Wooster

T0159671

CAMBRIDGE
UNIVERSITY PRESS

Shaftesbury Road, Cambridge CB2 8EA, United Kingdom

One Liberty Plaza, 20th Floor, New York, NY 10006, USA

477 Williamstown Road, Port Melbourne, VIC 3207, Australia

314–321, 3rd Floor, Plot 3, Splendor Forum, Jasola District Centre, New Delhi – 110025, India

103 Penang Road, #05–06/07, Visioncrest Commercial, Singapore 238467

Cambridge University Press is part of the University of Cambridge.

It furthers the University's mission by disseminating knowledge in the pursuit of education, learning and research at the highest international levels of excellence.

www.cambridge.org
Information on this title: www.cambridge.org/9781108948333

© Cambridge University Press & Assessment 2021

This publication is in copyright. Subject to statutory exception and to the provisions of relevant collective licensing agreements, no reproduction of any part may take place without the written permission of Cambridge University Press.

First published 1998
Second edition 2002
Third edition 2010
Fourth edition 2014
Fifth edition 2021

20 19 18 17 16 15 14 13 12 11 10 9 8 7 6

Printed in the Netherlands by Wilco BV

A catalogue record for this publication is available from the British Library

ISBN   978-1-108-94833-3   Practical Workbook with Digital Access (2 Years)

Additional resources for this publication at www.cambridge.org/9781108948333

NOTICE TO TEACHERS IN THE UK

It is illegal to reproduce any part of this work in material form (including photocopying and electronic storage) except under the following circumstances:

(i)   where you are abiding by a licence granted to your school or institution by the Copyright Licensing Agency;

(ii) where no such licence exists, or where you wish to exceed the terms of a licence, and you have gained the written permission of Cambridge University Press;

(iii) where you are allowed to reproduce without permission under the provisions of Chapter 3 of the Copyright, Designs and Patents Act 1988, which covers, for example, the reproduction of short passages within certain types of educational anthology and reproduction for the purposes of setting examination questions.

NOTICE TO TEACHERS

Cambridge International copyright material in this publication is reproduced under licence and remains the intellectual property of Cambridge Assessment International Education.

Cambridge International recommends that teachers consider using a range of teaching and learning resources in preparing learners for assessment, based on their own professional judgement of their students' needs.

DEDICATED TEACHER AWARDS

Teachers play an important part in shaping futures. Our Dedicated Teacher Awards recognise the hard work that teachers put in every day.

Thank you to everyone who nominated this year; we have been inspired and moved by all of your stories. Well done to all of our nominees for your dedication to learning and for inspiring the next generation of thinkers, leaders and innovators.

Congratulations to our incredible winner and finalists!

WINNER

Patricia Abril	Stanley Manaay	Tiffany Cavanagh	Helen Comerford	John Nicko Coyoca	Meera Rangarajan
New Cambridge School, Colombia	Salvacion National High School, Philippines	Trident College Solwezi, Zambia	Lumen Christi Catholic College, Australia	University of San Jose-Recoletos, Philippines	RBK International Academy, India

For more information about our dedicated teachers and their stories, go to
dedicatedteacher.cambridge.org

CAMBRIDGE
UNIVERSITY PRESS

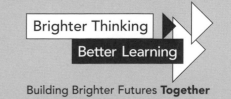

Brighter Thinking
Better Learning

Building Brighter Futures **Together**

> Contents

> How to use this series

We offer a comprehensive, flexible array of resources for the Cambridge IGCSE™ Chemistry syllabus. We provide targeted support and practice for the specific challenges we've heard that students face: learning science with English as a second language; learners who find the mathematical content within science difficult; and developing practical skills.

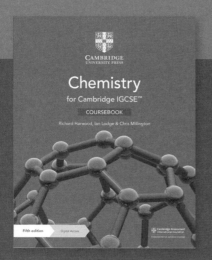

The coursebook provides coverage of the full Cambridge IGCSE Chemistry syllabus. Each chapter explains facts and concepts, and uses relevant real-world examples of scientific principles to bring the subject to life. Together with a focus on practical work and plenty of active learning opportunities, the coursebook prepares learners for all aspects of their scientific study. At the end of each chapter, examination-style questions offer practice opportunities for learners to apply their learning.

The digital teacher's resource contains detailed guidance for all topics of the syllabus, including common misconceptions identifying areas where learners might need extra support, as well as an engaging bank of lesson ideas for each syllabus topic. Differentiation is emphasised with advice for identification of different learner needs and suggestions of appropriate interventions to support and stretch learners. The teacher's resource also contains support for preparing and carrying out all the investigations in the practical workbook, including a set of sample results for when practicals aren't possible.

The teacher's resource also contains scaffolded worksheets and unit tests for each chapter. Answers for all components are accessible to teachers for free on the Cambridge Go platform.

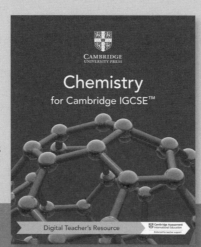

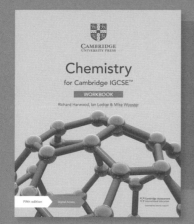

The skills-focused workbook has been carefully constructed to help learners develop the skills that they need as they progress through their Cambridge IGCSE Chemistry course, providing further practice of all the topics in the coursebook. A three-tier, scaffolded approach to skills development enables students to gradually progress through 'focus', 'practice' and 'challenge' exercises, ensuring that every learner is supported. The workbook enables independent learning and is ideal for use in class or as homework.

The practical workbook provides learners with additional opportunities for hands-on practical work, giving them full guidance and support that will help them to develop their investigative skills. These skills include planning investigations, selecting and handling apparatus, creating hypotheses, recording and displaying results, and analysing and evaluating data.

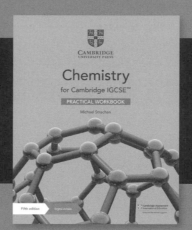

COMING SOON

Mathematics is an integral part of scientific study, and one that learners often find a barrier to progression in science. The Cambridge IGCSE Chemistry write-in maths skills workbook has been written in collaboration with the Association for Science Education, with each chapter focusing on several maths skills that students need to succeed in their Chemistry course.

Our research shows that English language skills are the single biggest barrier to students accessing international science. This write-in English language skills workbook contains exercises set within the context of Cambridge IGCSE Chemistry topics to consolidate understanding and embed practice in aspects of language central to the subject Activities range from practising using the passive form of the verbs in the context of electrolysis to the naming of chemical substances using common prefixes.

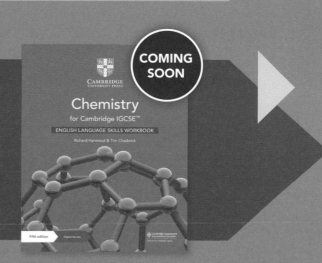

COMING SOON

> How to use this book

Throughout this book, you will notice lots of different features that will help your learning. These are explained below. Answers are accessible to teachers for free on the 'supporting resources' area of the Cambridge GO website.

KEY WORDS

Definitions for useful vocabulary are given at the start of each section. You will also find definitions for these words in the Glossary at the back of this book.

Supplement content: In the key word boxes, Supplement content is indicated with a large arrow, as in this example.

LEARNING INTENTIONS

These set the scene for each exercise, beginning with 'In this exercise you will:', and indicate the important concepts.

> In the learning intentions box, Supplement content is indicated with a large arrow and a darker background, as in this example.

TIPS

The information in these boxes will help you complete the exercises, and give you support in areas that you might find difficult.

Exercises

These help you to practise skills that are important for studying Cambridge IGCSE Chemistry.

Questions within exercises fall into one of three types:

- Focus questions will help build your basic skills.
- Practice questions provide more opportunities for practice, pushing your skills further.
- Challenge questions will stretch and challenge you even further. They may sometimes use unfamiliar contexts and ask you to apply your chemistry knowledge to these contexts in a logical way.

SELF/PEER ASSESSMENT

At the end of some exercises, you will find opportunities to help you assess your own work, or that of your classmates, and consider how you can improve the way you learn.

Supplement content

Where content is intended for students who are studying the Supplement content of the syllabus as well as the Core, this is indicated with the arrow and bar, as you can see on the left here.

> Introduction

This Cambridge IGCSE Chemistry Workbook has been written to help you increase your understanding of the topics covered in your Cambridge IGCSE Chemistry course. As you work through the book, chapter by chapter, you will develop the relevant scientific skills needed and gain the confidence to use them yourself. The exercises in this Workbook provide opportunities for you to practise the following skills:

- drawing graphs, reading scales, interpreting data and drawing conclusions

- using technical vocabulary correctly

- writing about the ideas you have been studying

- extending your knowledge to novel situations that you have not met before

- doing calculations, showing your working clearly

- planning and evaluating experiments.

The exercises in each chapter will help you develop these skills by applying them to new contexts. The chapters are arranged in the same order as the chapters in the Coursebook. It is not intended that you should necessarily do the exercises in the order printed, but that you should do them, as needed, during your course.

Each exercise has an introduction that outlines the skills you will be developing. Exercises progress through 'focus', 'practice' and 'challenge' stages. The 'focus' questions help to build your foundation skills before gradually giving you more opportunities for practice. The challenge questions aim to stretch you even further.

This Workbook is designed to support the Coursebook, with specially selected topics where learners would benefit from further opportunities to apply skills, such as application, analysis and evaluation in addition to developing knowledge and understanding. The Workbook does not cover all learning objectives in the Cambridge IGCSE Chemistry syllabus.

> Chapter 1

States of matter

> Changing physical state

> **KEY WORDS**
>
> **boiling:** the process of change from liquid to gas at the boiling point of the substance; a condition under which gas bubbles are able to form within a liquid – gas molecules escape from the body of the liquid, not just from its surface
>
> **freezing point:** the temperature at which a liquid turns into solid – it has the same value as the melting point; a pure substance has a sharp freezing point
>
> **melting point:** the temperature at which a solid turns into a liquid – it has the same value as the freezing point; a pure substance has a sharp melting point

Exercise 1.1

> **IN THIS EXERCISE YOU WILL:**
>
> - develop your understanding of the distinguishing properties of solids, liquids and gases
>
> - show how the properties of each state of matter are linked to the organisation of the particles present
>
> - use data on melting and boiling points to determine the physical state of a substance at a given temperature.

Focus

1   There are three states of matter, which have different basic physical properties. For all physical states, complete the sentences by adding two properties they show.

A solid has a fixed .... and ....

A liquid has a fixed .... but its .... changes to that of the container in which it is placed.

A gas has no fixed .... or .... A gas completely fills the container that it is in.

2   Complete Figure 1.1 to show how the particles of a substance are arranged in the three states of matter.

solid	liquid	gas

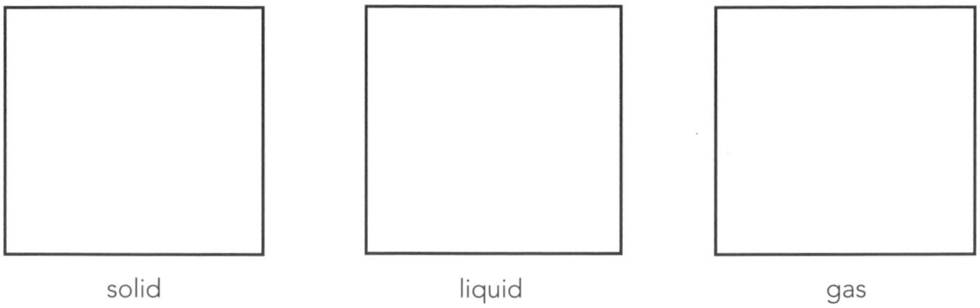

Figure 1.1: The three states of matter.

Practice

Question 2 illustrates the differences in structure and organisation of the particles in the three states. The differences can also be expressed in words. Table 1.1 describes the arrangement of the particles in four different substances A, B, C and D.

Substance	Distance between particles	Arrangement of particles	Movement of particles
A	Very far apart	Randomly arranged	Moving about with high speed
B	Very close together	Regularly ordered	Vibrating about fixed positions
C	Very far apart	Regularly ordered	Vibrating about fixed positions
D	Close together	Irregularly arranged	Moving about

Table 1.1: The arrangement and movement of particles in substances A, B, C and D.

3   Which of substances A, B, C and D is:

   a   a solid   ....

   b   unlikely to be a real substance   ....

   c   a gas   ....

   d   a liquid   ....

> **TIP**
>
> In a liquid, the particles are still close together. However, the particles are not regularly arranged and can move around and move past each other.

4   Changing the temperature can result in a substance changing its physical state. What are the changes of state A, B, C and D in Figure 1.2? (Note that sublimation is not required knowledge.)

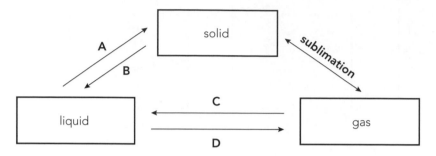

Figure 1.2: Changes of physical state.

A   ....

B   ....

C   ....

D   ....

Challenge

5   Use the data provided in Table 1.2 to answer the questions about the physical state of the substances listed when at a room temperature of 25 °C and at atmospheric pressure.

Substance	Melting point / °C	Boiling point / °C
Sodium	98	883
Radon	−71	−62
Ethanol	−117	78
Cobalt	1492	2900
Nitrogen	−210	−196
Propane	−188	−42
Ethanoic acid	16	118

Table 1.2: Melting points and boiling points of various substances.

a Which substance is a liquid over the smallest range of temperatures?

....

b Which two substances are gaseous at −50 °C?

.... and ....

c Which substance has the lowest freezing point?

....

d Which substance is liquid at 2500 °C?

....

e A sample of ethanoic acid was found to boil at 121 °C at atmospheric pressure. Use the information provided in Table 1.2 to comment on this result.

....

....

> **TIP**
>
> Be careful when dealing with temperatures below 0 °C, and remember that −100 °C is a higher temperature than −150 °C.

› Plotting a cooling curve

> **KEY WORDS**
>
> **evaporation:** a process occurring at the surface of a liquid, involving the change of state from a liquid into a vapour at a temperature below the boiling point
>
> **kinetic (particle) theory:** a theory which accounts for the bulk properties of the different states of matter in terms of the movement of particles (atoms or molecules) – the theory explains what happens during changes in physical state

Exercise 1.2

IN THIS EXERCISE YOU WILL:

- use data from an experiment to plot a cooling curve for a substance

- develop your understanding of the changes in organisation and movement of particles that take place as a substance changes state

> look at the changes in movement of particles in evaporation and boiling, and consider some unusual changes of state

> link the different changes of state to the kinetic (particle) theory of matter and explain the changes taking place.

Focus

A student carried out the following data-logging experiment as part of a project on changes of state. An organic crystalline solid was melted by placing it in a tube in a boiling water-bath. A temperature sensor was placed in the liquid.

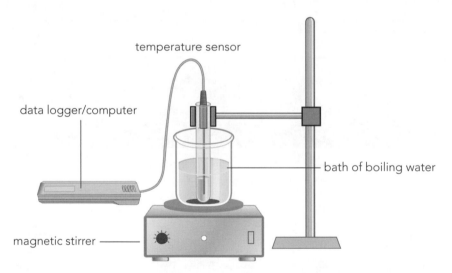

Figure 1.3: Using a temperature sensor to plot a cooling curve.

The student followed the temperature change as the liquid was allowed to cool. The data shown in Table 1.3 are taken from the computer record of the temperature change as the liquid cooled to room temperature.

Time / minutes	0	0.5	1.0	1.5	2.0	2.2	2.4	2.6	2.8	3.0	3.5	4.0	4.5	5.0
Temperature / °C	96.1	89.2	85.2	82.0	80.9	80.7	80.6	80.6	80.5	80.3	78.4	74.2	64.6	47.0

Table 1.3: Results for cooling curve experiment.

6   On the grid provided, plot a graph of the temperature change that took place in this experiment.

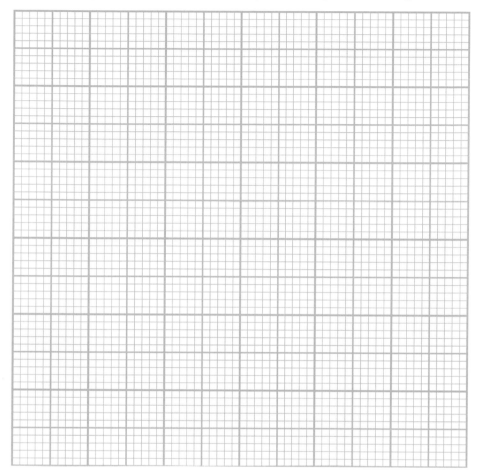

7   The student decided to carry out the experiment using a compound that has a melting point greater than 100 °C. What change would she need to make to carry out the experiment?

....

8   What change is taking place over the third minute of the experiment?

....

Practice

9   Why does the temperature remain almost constant over this period of time (the third minute of the experiment)? When giving your answer, think about how the organisation of the molecules of the substance is changing.

....

....

(continued)

....

....

....

....

10 Another student carried out a similar experiment to demonstrate the cooling curve for paraffin wax.

    a   In the space provided, sketch the shape of the graph you would expect the student to produce.

    b   Explain why you have chosen the shape for the curve you drew in **a**.

....

....

> ### TIP
>
> Pure substances have definite, precise melting points and boiling points. When a substance contains impurities, the melting and boiling points change and become less precise (spread over a range of temperatures).

Challenge

11 Experiments that allow a student to plot a cooling curve can be reversed, and a heating curve can be plotted instead. Figure 1.4 shows the heating curve for a pure substance. The temperature rises with time as the substance is heated.

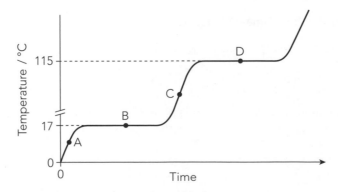

Figure 1.4: A heating curve for a pure substance.

a What physical state(s) is the substance in at points A, B, C and D?

A ....

B ....

C ....

D ....

b What is the melting point of the substance?

....

c What is the boiling point of the substance?

....

d How does the temperature change while the substance is changing state?

....

e The substance is not water. How do you know this from the graph?

....

12 Dry ice is the name given to the solid form of carbon dioxide. Dry ice is used in commercial refrigeration and to create spectacular and misty stage effects. The surface of dry ice at atmospheric pressure is different from that of ordinary water ice as there is no liquid film on it.

a If you gently shake a fire extinguisher filled with carbon dioxide (Figure 1.5), you will feel the presence of liquid within the extinguisher. What conditions within the extinguisher mean that the carbon dioxide is liquid?

....

....

Figure 1.5: A carbon dioxide fire extinguisher.

b Frost is ice crystals that form on surfaces when conditions are very cold. Using the words provided, complete the following paragraph about a particular type of frost known as hoar frost.

colder   crystals   humid   ice   liquid   surrounding   white

Hoar frost is a powdery .... frost caused when solid ....

forms from .... air. The solid surface on which it is formed must be

.... than the .... air. Water vapour is deposited on a surface

as fine ice .... without going through the .... phase.

c For most substances, the change from a solid to a gas involves a liquid phase. The final stage of this, from liquid to gas, takes place by evaporation and/or boiling. Use the ideas of kinetic (particle) theory to explain the difference between these two processes.

Evaporation:

....

....

....

....

....

....

Boiling:

....

....

....

....

....

....

SELF-ASSESSMENT

Use the checklist below to give yourself a mark for the graph you drew in question **6**.

For each point, award yourself:

2 marks   if you did it really well

1 mark   if you made a good attempt at it and partly succeeded

0 marks   if you did not try to do it, or did not succeed

Then ask your teacher to mark you on the skills as well.

Checklist	Marks awarded	
	You	Your teacher
Have you drawn the axes with a ruler, using most of the width and height of the grid?		
Have you used a good scale for the *x*-axis and the *y*-axis, which goes up in easily managed units (1 minute, 2 minutes, etc.)? (Note that the axes do not necessarily need to start at the origin (0,0).)		
Have you labelled the axes correctly? Have you given the correct units for the scales on both axes?		
Have you plotted each point precisely and correctly?		
Have you used a small neat cross or encircled dot for each point?		
Have you drawn a single, clear best-fit line through each set of points?		
Have you ignored any anomalous (unexpected) results when drawing the line through each set of points?		
Total (out of 14):		

Your total score will reflect how clear and well-presented your graph is. You should be able to deduce reliable information from your graph.

Look at where you scored yourself two marks and where you gave yourself less than that. What did you do well, and what aspects will you focus on next time? Having thought about your assessment, talk it through with your teacher to gain further advice on areas that would help you improve your presentation of graphical data.

> Dissolving and diffusion

KEY WORD

diffusion: the process by which different fluids mix as a result of the random motions of their particles

Exercise 1.3

IN THIS EXERCISE YOU WILL:

- consider how the process of diffusion explains how a solid can dissolve in a liquid

- examine how diffusion in a liquid or gas results from the spreading of particles to fill the space available to them

> consider the relationship between the rate of diffusion in gases and their molecular mass.

Focus

13 A student placed some crystals of potassium manganate(VII) at the bottom of a beaker of distilled water. She then left the contents of the beaker to stand for one hour.

Figure 1.6 shows what she saw during the experiment. After one hour, the student observed that all the solid crystals had disappeared and the solution was purple throughout.

distilled water

purple crystals

at start   after 15 minutes   after 1 hour

Figure 1.6: Crystals of potassium manganate(VII) placed in water.

a Use the ideas of the kinetic (particle) theory to explain the student's observations.

You may wish to use some or all of the following phrases in constructing your answer.

> crystal surface   evenly spread   particles move
>
> solid dissolves completely   spread out   the crystals are soluble

....

....

....

....

....

b If the student had used warm water at 50 °C, would the observations have taken place in a longer or shorter time? Explain your answer.

....

....

....

Practice

14 Ammonium chloride is often given as an example of a compound that can change from a solid to a gas, without passing through a liquid stage (Figure 1.7). The white solid enters directly into the vapour state when heated, but the solid then reforms on the cooler upper part of the tube.

Figure 1.7: Heating ammonium chloride.

In fact, these changes in state of ammonium chloride involve two chemical reactions. The first reaction is the thermal decomposition of the solid ammonium chloride. The products are two gases: ammonia and hydrogen chloride.

a Write a word equation for the decomposition of ammonium chloride.

....

b   In the cooler part of the tube the two gases react to form ammonium chloride.

Complete the following chemical equation for this reaction (include the state symbol for the missing reactant).

$NH_3(g)$ + ... $\rightarrow NH_4Cl(s)$

Challenge

15   Figure 1.8 shows a laboratory demonstration of this reaction. The apparatus is arranged so that the two gases, ammonia and hydrogen chloride, diffuse towards each other in a sealed tube.

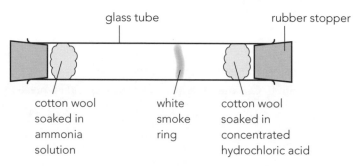

glass tube   rubber stopper

cotton wool   white   cotton wool
soaked in   smoke   soaked in
ammonia   ring   concentrated
solution   hydrochloric acid

Figure 1.8: Demonstration of the different rates of diffusion for gases.

Where the gases meet within the sealed tube, they react to form a white smoke ring of ammonium chloride.

a   The white solid forms nearer the end of the tube containing the concentrated hydrochloric acid. Explain why.

....

....

....

b   If the distance between the cotton wool balls is 45 cm, approximately how far along from the end of the tube containing the ammonia will the white ring form?

....

....

Table 1.4 shows the formulae and relative molecular masses of four different gases.

Gas	Formula	Relative molecular mass (M_r)
Oxygen	O_2	32
Hydrogen	H_2	2
Chlorine	Cl_2	71
Methane	CH_4	16

Table 1.4: Formulae and relative molecular masses of several gases.

c List the four gases in order of their rate of diffusion (with the quickest first).

....

> **TIP**
>
> When asked to list things in increasing or decreasing order, make sure you understand in which order to put the items. Make sure you use the 'greater than' (>) and 'less than' (<) symbols correctly.

d A gas, G, diffuses slower than methane, but faster than oxygen. What can you say about the relative molecular mass of G?

....

....

16 Complete the paragraphs using the words provided.

different   diffuse   diffusion   gas   inversely   lattice

molecular   particles   random   spread   temperature   vibrate

The kinetic model states that the .... in a liquid and in a .... are

constantly moving. In a gas, the particles are far apart from each other and their movement

is said to be .... The particles in a solid are held in fixed positions in a

regular .... In a solid, the particles can only .... about their

fixed positions.

Liquids and gases are fluids. When particles move in a fluid, they can collide with each other.

When they collide, they bounce off each other in .... directions. If two gases or

liquids are mixed, the different types of particle .... out and get mixed up. This

process is called ....

In gases at the same ...., particles that have a lower mass move faster than

particles with higher mass. This means that the lighter particles will spread and mix more

quickly. The lighter particles are said to .... faster than the heavier particles.

When gaseous molecules diffuse, the rate at which they do so is .... related to the

relative .... mass (M_r) of the gas.

> Chapter 2

Atomic structure

> The structure of the atom

KEY WORDS

electron: a subatomic particle with negligible mass and a charge of −1; electrons are present in all atoms, located in shells (energy levels) outside the nucleus

electronic configuration: a shorthand method of describing the arrangement of electrons within the electron shells (or energy levels) of an atom; also referred to as electronic structure

electron shells (energy levels): (of electrons) the allowed energies of electrons in atoms – electrons fill these shells (or levels) starting with the one closest to the nucleus

neutron: an uncharged subatomic particle present in the nuclei of atoms – a neutron has a mass of 1 relative to a proton

nucleon: a particle present in the nucleus of an atom

proton: a subatomic particle with a relative atomic mass of 1 and a charge of +1, found in the nucleus of all atoms

subatomic particles: very small particles – protons, neutrons and electrons – from which all atoms are made (Note: the term subatomic particles, while a useful description, is not an essential term to learn.)

Exercise 2.1

IN THIS EXERCISE YOU WILL:

- see how the structure of any atom is defined by its proton (atomic) number and mass (nucleon) number

- learn how the electrons in an atom are organised in shells around the nucleus

- find out how the electronic configuration of an atom relates to its position in the Periodic Table of elements.

Focus

Dalton's atomic theory had originally suggested that atoms were the indivisible particles from which the elements were made. However, we have since found that atoms are themselves made up of subatomic particles. Each element is made up of atoms with a different characteristic number of these particles.

1   Complete the passage using the words provided. Words may be used once, more than once or not at all.

electrons   isotopes   neutrons   nucleon

nucleus   proton   protons   shells

Atoms are made up of three different particles:

*   ...., which are positively charged

*   ...., which have no charge

*   ...., which are negatively charged.

The negatively charged particles are arranged in different .... (energy levels)

around the .... of the atom. The particles with a negligible mass are

the .... All atoms of the same element contain the same number of

.... and .... Atoms of the same element with different numbers

of .... are known as ....

2   An atom of lithium has three protons and a nucleon number of 7.

a   How many electrons are in the lithium atom? ....

b   How many neutrons does lithium have? ....

c   What is the mass number of this lithium atom? ....

d   Describe the lithium atom in the format that uses two numbers and the symbol for

the element. ....

Practice

3   This part of the exercise is concerned with electronic configurations and the structure of the Periodic Table. Complete the passage with the missing words or numbers.

The electrons in an atom are arranged in a series of .... around the

central nucleus. These shells are also called .... levels. In an atom, the shell

.... to the nucleus fills first, then the next shell, and so on. There is room for:

*   up to .... electrons in the first shell

*   up to .... electrons in the second shell

*   up to .... electrons in the third shell.

(For elements up to calcium, Z = 20, there are 18 electrons in total when the three shells are full.)

The elements in the Periodic Table are organised in the same way as the electrons fill the shells.

Shells fill from .... to .... across the .... of the Periodic Table.

- The first shell fills up first, from .... to helium.

- The second shell fills next, from lithium to ....

- Eight .... go into the third shell, from sodium to argon.

- Then the fourth shell starts to fill, from potassium.

> **TIP**
>
> The electronic configuration of an atom can be given either as the numbers in a list, starting from the first shell (e.g. 2,8,4 for silicon) or the structure can be drawn as a diagram where electrons are shown orbiting the nucleus of the atom. Remember, you are only expected to be able to give the electronic configurations of the first 20 elements in the Periodic Table at IGCSE.

Challenge

4   Use the Periodic Table to help you name the following elements.

   a   the element with an electronic configuration of 2,8,2 ....

   b   the element with an electronic configuration of 2,7 ....

   c   the element with an electronic configuration of 2,8,8,1 ....

5   Give the names and electronic configurations of the following.

   a   the element in Group III, Period 2

   ....

   b   the element in Group V, Period 3

   ....

6   Complete the electronic configurations of the Group II elements in Table 2.1.

Beryllium	2,2	Magnesium	.....,8,.....	Calcium	2,8,.....,.....

Table 2.1: The electronic configurations of some Group II elements.

TIP

Use the Periodic Table at the back of this Workbook to help you work out the composition of subatomic particles in any atom. For example, magnesium is the 12th atom in the Periodic Table, so it must have 12 protons and 12 electrons in its atoms.

SELF-ASSESSMENT

Which parts of this exercise did you find easy and which parts were difficult? Put a tick (✓) or cross (✗) next to the following statements.

- I feel confident defining a proton, a neutron and an electron. ☐

- I feel confident describing the atomic structure of the first 20 elements of the Periodic Table. ☐

- I can clearly describe the relationship between atomic structure and the Periodic Table. ☐

> Subatomic organisation, properties and isotopes

KEY WORDS

isotopes: atoms of the same element which have the same proton number but a different nucleon number; they have different numbers of neutrons in their nuclei; some isotopes are radioactive because their nuclei are unstable (radioisotopes)

relative atomic mass (A_r): the average mass of naturally occurring atoms of an element on a scale where the carbon-12 atom has a mass of exactly 12 units

Exercise 2.2

IN THIS EXERCISE YOU WILL:

- learn that the properties of an atom are dependent on the organisation of its subatomic particles

- learn that isotopes of an element have the same number of protons but different numbers of neutrons and how a particular isotope can be represented symbolically

> learn that the isotopes of an element all have the same chemical properties

> calculate the relative atomic mass of an element.

Focus

7 Table 2.2 gives details of the atomic structure of five atoms A, B, C, D and E.

    a Complete the table to show the electronic configuration of each of the atoms.

Atom	Proton number	Electronic configuration			
		1st shell	2nd shell	3rd shell	4th shell
A	2				
B	5				
C	13				
D	15				
E	19				

Table 2.2: Table of electronic configurations.

    b How many of these atoms are of elements in the second period of the Periodic Table?

        ....

    c Which two atoms belong to elements in the same group?

        ....

    d How many electrons does atom C have which would be involved in chemical bonding?

        ....

    e Figure 2.1 shows the arrangement of electrons in the shells (energy levels) of atom B. Using this as a guide, draw a diagram to show the arrangement of the electrons in atom D in the space provided.

           Atom B   **Atom D**

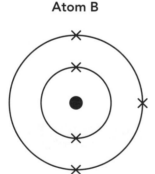

Figure 2.1: The electron arrangements of atoms B and D.

Practice

8 In 1986, an explosion at Chernobyl in Ukraine released a radioactive cloud containing various radioactive isotopes. Three of these isotopes are given in Table 2.3. Use the Periodic Table to answer the following questions about them.

Element	Mass (nucleon) number
Strontium	90
Iodine	131
Caesium	137

Table 2.3: Isotopes released at Chernobyl.

a How many electrons are in one atom of strontium-90? ....

b How many protons are in one atom of iodine-131? ....

c How many neutrons are in one atom of iodine-131? ....

d How many neutrons are in one atom of caesium-137? ....

e Define an isotope.

....

....

TIP

Any atom is electrically neutral. The two defining numbers the proton (atomic) number and the mass (nucleon) number for any atom can be used to work out the composition of subatomic particles.

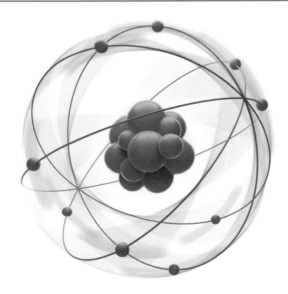

9   Figure 2.2 shows the structures of five atoms A, B, C, D and E.

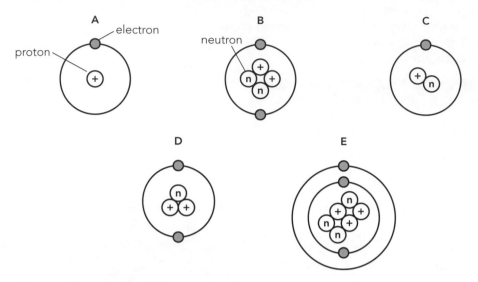

Figure 2.2: Atomic structure of five atoms A–E.

Answer the following questions about these atoms. Each structure may be used once, more than once, or not at all.

a   Which structure has a mass number of 4? ....

b   Which structure represents the atom of a metal? ....

c   Which two atoms are isotopes of each other? ....

d   Which structures are isotopes of helium? ....

Challenge

The characteristic properties of an atom are related to the way in which the subatomic particles are organised within that atom. Properties such as whether an atom is radioactive, the type of bonds it makes, its chemical reactivity and its position in the Periodic Table are all dependent on this organisation.

10 The modern view of the structure of the atom stems from experiments using α-particles (helium nuclei) fired at a sheet of gold foil from a radioactive source. Detectors analysed the direction of the particles as they passed through the foil. The design of the experiment is summarised in Figure 2.3.

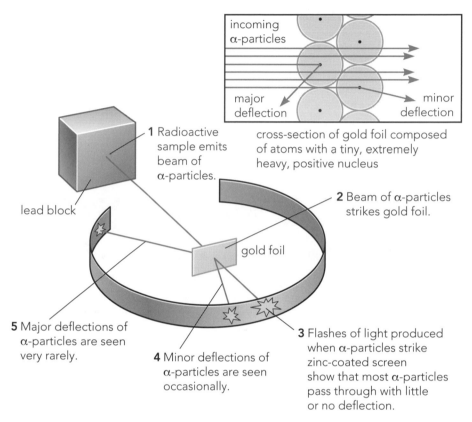

1 Radioactive sample emits beam of α-particles.

cross-section of gold foil composed of atoms with a tiny, extremely heavy, positive nucleus

lead block

2 Beam of α-particles strikes gold foil.

gold foil

5 Major deflections of α-particles are seen very rarely.

4 Minor deflections of α-particles are seen occasionally.

3 Flashes of light produced when α-particles strike zinc-coated screen show that most α-particles pass through with little or no deflection.

Figure 2.3: The Geiger and Marsden experiment. (Note that the Geiger-Marsden experiment is not required knowledge.)

a α-particles are helium nuclei. What is the composition of an α-particle and its charge?

Protons: ....

Neutrons: ....

Charge: ....

b Gold foil is a solid metal. How are the atoms of gold arranged in the foil?

....

....

c What did the fact that most of the α-particles passed through the foil suggest about the structure of the atoms?

....

....

   d Remarkably, some α-particles were repelled back in the direction from which they came. What part of the structure of the atom did this observation suggest the particles had hit? Why were these particles repelled backwards?

   ....

   ....

   ....

11 The isotopes of some elements, such as carbon-14, can be of use in biochemical and medical research. Because they are radioactive, they can be used by scientists to track the synthesis and use of compounds important in the chemistry of cells and tissues.

   a Complete Table 2.4 about the isotopes of some common elements, making deductions from the information given. For each element, the second isotope is a radioisotope used in research.

Isotope	Name of element	Atomic number	Mass (nucleon) number	Number of		
				protons	neutrons	electrons
$^{12}_{6}C$	Carbon	6	12	6	6	6
$^{14}_{6}C$						
$^{1}_{1}H$			1			
$^{3}_{1}H$	Hydrogen (tritium)					
$^{31}_{15}P$		15	31			
$^{32}_{15}P$						
$^{127}_{53}I$	Iodine			53		53
$^{131}_{53}I$				53		

Table 2.4: The isotopes of certain elements.

b Researchers are able to use these radioisotopes to study the chemistry of cells because these atoms have the same chemical properties as the non-radioactive atoms. Why are the chemical properties of all isotopes of the same element identical?

....

....

....

....

....

....

c Rhenium is one of the rarest elements in the Earth's crust and was the second-last element with a stable isotope (rhenium-185) to be discovered. The other isotope of rhenium (rhenium-187) is radioactive. The relative abundance of rhenium-185 is 37.4%. Calculate the relative atomic mass (A_r) of rhenium.

....

....

....

....

....

....

....

> **TIP**
>
> When calculating the relative atomic mass (A_r) of an element, remember to take into account all the isotopes, calculate the total mass of 100 atoms, and then divide by 100 to find the mean average mass of one atom.

Chapter 3

Chemical bonding

> Elements, compounds and mixtures

KEY WORDS

compound: a substance formed by the chemical combination of two or more elements in fixed proportions

element: a substance which cannot be further divided into simpler substances by chemical methods: all the atoms of an element contain the same number of protons

mixture: two or more substances mixed together but not chemically combined – the substances can be separated by physical means

Exercise 3.1

IN THIS EXERCISE YOU WILL:

- review the key differences between elements, compounds and mixtures

- understand the representation of these different substances in diagrams.

Focus

1 Using the words provided, complete Table 3.1 to show the difference between a compound and a mixture. Some words may be used more than once.

any   combined   definite   different

elements   physical   present   properties   separated

Compound	Mixture
The .... cannot be .... by .... methods.	The substances in it can be .... by .... methods.
The properties are .... from those of the .... that went to make it.	The substances .... still show the .... that they have when by themselves.
The elements are .... in a .... proportion by mass.	The substances can be .... in .... proportion by mass.

Table 3.1: A comparison of chemical compounds and mixtures.

Practice

2 The following is a list of everyday substances. Some of these are chemical compounds, others are mixtures.

air   brass   carbon dioxide   copper sulfate

distilled water   hydrochloric acid solution   lemonade

seawater   sodium chloride

Which of these substances are:

a   compounds?

....

....

b   mixtures?

....

....

3   Figure 3.1 shows six different substances. State which are pure elements, pure compounds or mixtures. Each circle represents an atom.

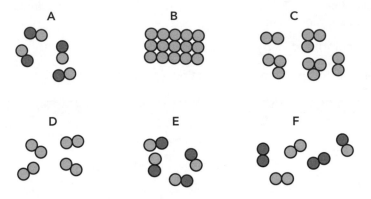

Figure 3.1: Arrangement of atoms in six different structures.

A   ....   B   C   ....

D   ....   E   ....   F   ....

Challenge

4   The reaction between sodium and chlorine is described in the following paragraph.

Sodium is a silvery-grey metal that reacts violently with water. Chlorine is a green gas that is toxic and dissolves in water to give a weakly acidic solution. When sodium reacts with chlorine, heat is given out and a white powder (sodium chloride) is formed. Sodium chloride dissolves in water to give a neutral solution.

What information in this paragraph tells us that sodium chloride is a compound, and not a mixture?

....

....

....

....

5   Iron is a grey magnetic metal that reacts with hydrochloric acid to produce hydrogen gas. Sulfur is a yellow non-metal that does not react with acids.

Powders of these two elements can be mixed and heated together in a test-tube. The mixture glows red on heating and continues to do this even when removed from the Bunsen burner flame.

The black powder produced after heating the mixture is not magnetic and reacts with hydrochloric acid to give a smelly gas, hydrogen sulfide.

Use these observations to answer the following questions.

a   State three differences between the two elements iron and sulfur.

....

....

....

b   Explain why the fact that the mixture continues to glow with heat when removed from the flame is important.

....

....

c   Give two pieces of evidence that a compound has been formed by heating the powders together.

....

....

....

> Covalent bonding

KEY WORDS

covalent bonding: chemical bonding formed by the sharing of one or more pairs of electrons between two atoms

displayed formula: a representation of the structure of a compound which shows all the atoms and bonds in the molecule

Exercise 3.2

IN THIS EXERCISE YOU WILL:

- describe how to draw the structures of simple covalent molecules
- draw dot-and-cross diagrams of the bonding in covalent molecules
- sketch diagrams showing the sharing of electrons between atoms to form covalent bonds.

Focus

6 Many covalent compounds exist as simple molecules where the atoms are joined together with single or double bonds. A covalent bond, made up of a shared pair of electrons, is often represented by a short straight line. Complete Table 3.2 by filling in the blank spaces.

Name of compound	Formula	Displayed formula	Molecular model
Hydrogen chloride	....	H—Cl	
Water	H_2O		
Ammonia	....		
....	CH_4		
Ethene	....		
....	....	O=C=O	

Table 3.2: The structure of some simple covalent molecules.

TIP

When drawing the displayed formula of a molecule it is important to show all the bonds whether they are single, double or even triple bonds.

Practice

7   Complete Table 3.3 by drawing dot-and-cross diagrams and displayed formulae to represent the bonding in the following simple molecular compounds. In the dot-and-cross diagrams, show only the outer shells of the atoms involved.

Molecule	Dot-and-cross diagram	Displayed formula
Ammonia (NH_3)		
Water (H_2O)		
Hydrogen chloride (HCl)		
Ethane (C_2H_6)		

Table 3.3: Diagrams representing the covalent bonding in different simple molecules.

> # Challenge

8   Complete Table 3.4 by drawing dot-and-cross and displayed formulae to represent the bonding in the following more complex molecular elements and compounds, some of which involve multiple bonding.

Molecule	Dot-and-cross diagram	Displayed formula
Nitrogen (N_2)		
Ethene (C_2H_4)		
Methanol (CH_3OH)		
Ethanoic acid (CH_3COOH)		

Table 3.4: The covalent bonding in some elements and compounds.

PEER ASSESSMENT

Share your drawings with a partner and check that they can understand what you have drawn. Ask them to use the following checklist:

☐   A correct dot-and-cross diagram and displayed formula have been drawn for each of the molecular compounds.

☐   The dot-and-cross diagrams clearly show the bonding in a molecule.

☐   Only the outer electrons have been included.

Discuss the checklist with your partner. Is there anything you could improve upon next time you draw these diagrams?

> Giant ionic and metallic lattices

KEY WORDS

anion: a negative ion which would be attracted to the anode in electrolysis

cation: a positive ion which would be attracted to the cathode in electrolysis

ductile: the word used to describe a substance that can be drawn out into a wire

giant ionic lattice (structure): a lattice held together by the electrostatic forces of attraction between positive and negative ions

metallic bonding: an electrostatic force of attraction between the mobile 'sea' of electrons and the regular array of positive metal ions within a solid metal

'sea' of delocalised electrons: term used for the free, mobile electrons between the positive ions in a metallic lattice

Exercise 3.3

IN THIS EXERCISE YOU WILL:

- describe the nature of ionic bonding and the properties of ionic compounds

> describe the nature of metallic bonding

> relate the nature of the type of bond formed to explain some of the physical properties of the substances involved.

Focus

9   Figure 3.2 shows a model of the structure of sodium chloride and similar ionic crystals. The ions are arranged in a regular lattice structure of alternating positive and negative ions, known as a giant ionic lattice.

Figure 3.2: A giant ionic lattice.

a   How does the electronic configuration of a sodium cation differ from that of a sodium atom?

....

b How does the electronic configuration of a chloride anion differ from that of a chlorine atom?

....

c Draw a dot-and-cross diagram to show the ions in sodium chloride.

d What type of forces of attraction hold the structure of sodium chloride together?

....

e Why does sodium chloride have a high melting point?

....

> **TIP**
>
> Ionic compounds do not conduct electricity when solid as the ions present are not free to move; they can only vibrate about fixed points in the structure.

Practice

10 The boxes contain properties of ionic compounds and their explanations. Draw lines to link each property box with the correct explanation.

Property	Explanation
A solution of an ionic compound in water is a good conductor of electricity. These ionic substances are called electrolytes.	The ions in the giant ionic structure always have the same regular arrangement (see Figure 3.2).
Ionic crystals have a regular shape. The crystals of each solid ionic compound are the same shape. The angles between the faces of the crystal are always the same, whatever the size of the crystal.	Strong attraction between the positive and negative ions holds the giant ionic structure together. A lot of energy is needed to break down the regular arrangement of ions.
Ionic compounds have relatively high melting points.	In a molten ionic compound, the positive and negative ions can move – the ions can move to the electrodes when a voltage is applied.
A molten ionic compound (i.e. an ionic compound heated above its melting point) is a good conductor of electricity.	In a solution of an ionic compound, the positive metal ions and the negative non-metal ions can move – these ions can move to the electrodes when a voltage is applied.

Challenge

11 a   Complete Figure 3.3 to show the nature of metallic bonding.

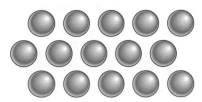

Figure 3.3: Metallic bonding.

_____

b   Use the information from your diagram to explain the following properties of metals.

i   Many metals have a high melting temperature.

....

....

ii   Metals are ductile.

....

....

iii   All metals conduct electricity.

....

....

> Giant covalent structures

KEY WORDS

giant covalent structures: a substance where large numbers of atoms are held together by covalent bonds forming a strong lattice structure

Exercise 3.4

IN THIS EXERCISE YOU WILL:

- describe the covalent structures of diamond and graphite
- relate the structures of diamond and graphite to their physical properties

> describe the structure of silicon(IV) oxide

> compare the similarities between the structures of diamond and silicon(IV) oxide.

Focus

12 Table 3.5 contains observations and explanations for the structures of diamond and graphite. Complete the table by filling in the gaps. The first section of the table has been completed for you; other sections are only partly complete.

Observation	Explanation
Diamond is a very hard substance …	… because all the atoms in the structure are joined by strong covalent bonds.
Diamond does not conduct electricity …	… because ....
Graphite is	… because the layers in the structure are only held together by weak forces.
....	… because there are some free electrons that are able to move between the layers to carry the current.

Table 3.5: The properties of diamond and graphite.

Practice

13 Graphite is one of the crystalline forms of carbon. Two of the distinctive properties of graphite are:

- it conducts electricity even though it is a non-metal
- it can act as a lubricant even though it has a giant covalent structure.

Give a brief explanation of these properties in the light of the structure of graphite.

a Graphite as an electrical conductor

....

....

....

b Graphite as a lubricant

....

....

....

Challenge

14 Silicon(IV) oxide is a very common compound in the crust of the Earth. It has a giant covalent structure similar to diamond. Summarise the features of the structure of silicon(IV) oxide (silica), as shown in Figure 3.4, by completing the following statements.

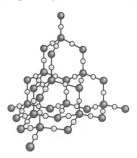

Figure 3.4: The structure of silicon(IV) oxide.

a   The strong bonds between the atoms are .... bonds.

b   In the crystal, there are two oxygen atoms for every silicon atom, so the formula is

   ....

c   The atoms of the lattice are organised in a .... arrangement like diamond, with a silicon atom at the centre of each ....

d   This is an example of a .... structure.

e   Each oxygen atom forms .... covalent bonds.

f   Each silicon atom forms .... covalent bonds.

15 Sand is a powder of silicon(IV) oxide (sometimes called silica or silicon dioxide). Its structure is shown in Figure 3.4. Complete the following statements about the structure of silicon(IV) oxide by deleting the incorrect words.

Silicon(IV) oxide occurs naturally as **mud / sand**. It has a giant **covalent / electrostatic** structure very similar to **graphite / diamond**. Such a structure can also be described as a giant **molecular / ionic** structure as all the atoms in the crystal are joined together by covalent bonds.

Each silicon atom is bonded to **four / two** oxygen atoms, while each oxygen atom is linked covalently to **four / two** silicon atoms. The oxygen atoms are arranged **hexagonally / tetrahedrally** around the silicon atoms.

The fact that all the atoms are bonded together in a **two-dimensional / three-dimensional** structure like **graphite / diamond** means that silicon(IV) oxide has similar physical properties to **graphite / diamond**. Silica is very **hard / slippery** and has a **low / high** melting point. All the outer electrons of the atoms in the structure are used in making the covalent bonds between the atoms. This means that silicon(IV) oxide **does / does not** conduct electricity. There are no electrons free to carry the current through the crystal.

> Chapter 4

Chemical formulae and equations

> The formulae of compounds

KEY WORDS

empirical formula: a formula for a compound which shows the simplest ratio of atoms present

molecular formula: a formula that shows the actual number of atoms of each element present in a molecule of the compound

Exercise 4.1

IN THIS EXERCISE YOU WILL:

- construct the formulae of ionic and covalent compounds

> show the difference between the molecular and empirical formula of a compound.

Focus

1   How many atoms of the different elements are there in the formulae of the following compounds?

   a   Nitric acid, HNO_3 ....

   b   Copper nitrate, $Cu(NO_3)_2$ ....

   c   Ammonium sulfate, $(NH_4)_2SO_4$ ....

   d   Potassium manganate(VII), $KMnO_4$ ....

2 a Complete Figure 4.1 by adding the valencies (combining power) of the atoms shown. (The term 'valency' is not required knowledge, but is a useful concept for working out the number of bonds an atom can form.)

Figure 4.1: A section of the Periodic Table.

b Which atoms in Figure 4.1 lose electrons when they form ions?

....

c Which atoms in Figure 4.1 gain electrons when they form ions?

....

d Name two atoms in Figure 4.1 that share electrons when they form compounds.

....

3 Write the formulae of the following compounds by balancing (or crossing over) the valencies. Use the position of the element in the Periodic Table to help you remember its valency.

a a compound of H and S ....

b a compound of B and O ....

c a compound of C and S ....

d the simplest compound of N and H ....

Practice

4 Lactose (a sugar), $C_{12}H_{22}O_{11}$, is sometimes used instead of charcoal in fireworks.

State the total number of atoms present in a molecule of lactose.

....

5 Atoms of elements P, Q and R have 16, 17 and 19 electrons, respectively. The atoms of argon have 18 electrons.

Predict the formulae of the compounds formed by the combination of the elements:

a P and R ....

b Q and R ....

c Q with itself ....

In each of the three cases shown in **a–c**, name the type of chemical bond formed.

i ....

ii ....

iii ....

> **TIP**
>
> The symbols of the elements that normally exist as diatomic molecules can be remembered by the memory aid: **I H**ave **N**o **Br**ight **O**r **Cl**ever **F**riends.

> Challenge

6 Using information from your completed Periodic Table in Figure 4.1, write the formulae of the following ionic compounds and state which ions are present in each compound.

   a a compound of Mg and Br

   ....

   b a compound of Ca and N

   ....

   c a compound of Al and O

   ....

7 A molecule of compound Y contains the following atoms bonded covalently together:

- 2 atoms of carbon (C)
- 2 atoms of oxygen (O)
- 4 atoms of hydrogen (H)

   a What is the molecular formula of a molecule of Y? ....

   b What is the empirical formula of Y? ....

8 Complete the paragraphs about the formulae of compounds using the words provided (some words may be used more than once).

atoms　bonded　carbon　compound　dividing

empirical　hydrogen　ionic　molecular　ratio

The formula of a simple molecular .... shows exactly how many atoms are

.... together in each molecule. For example, ethane has two ....

and six .... atoms, so its formula is C_2H_6. This is the .... formula

for ethane. This formula can be simplified to CH_3 by .... through by 2.

CH_3 is the .... formula of ethane.

The formulae used for giant covalent and .... compounds are the simplest

.... of the different .... or ions in each compound. These formulae

are known as the .... formulae of these types of compounds.

TIP

Remember the difference between the molecular formula and the empirical formula for a simple covalent compound. You should always use the molecular formula in equations.

> # Formulae and equations

KEY WORDS

balanced chemical (symbol) equation: a summary of a chemical reaction using chemical formulae – the total number of any of the atoms involved is the same on both the reactant and product sides of the equation

compound ion: an ion made up of several different atoms covalently bonded together and with an overall charge (can also be called a molecular ion; negatively charged compound ions containing oxygen can be called oxyanions)

ionic equation: the simplified equation for a reaction involving ionic substances: only those ions which actually take part in the reaction are shown

state symbols: symbols used to show the physical state of the reactants and products in a chemical reaction: they are s (solid), l (liquid), g (gas) and aq (in solution in water)

word equation: a summary of a chemical reaction using the chemical names of the reactants and products

Exercise 4.2

IN THIS EXERCISE YOU WILL:

- write word equations and balanced chemical (symbol) equations for chemical reactions

- use state symbols to add to the information given in an equation

⟩ construct formulae, from ions, in which the charges balance so that the overall formula has no charge

⟩ convert symbol equations into ionic equations to show the ions taking part in a reaction.

Focus

9 The 'model equation' shown describes the combustion of methane (Figure 4.2).

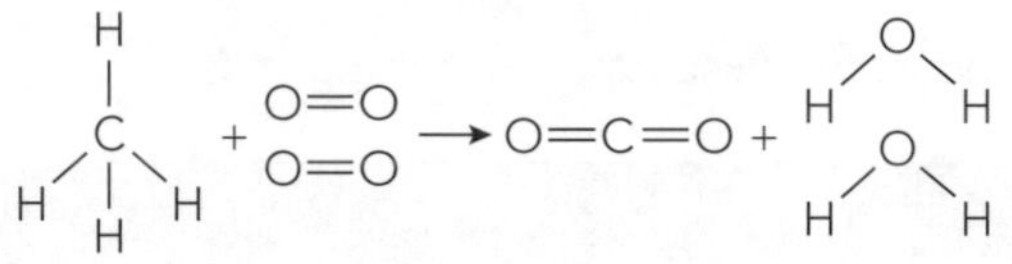

Figure 4.2: The combustion of methane.

a Write the word equation for this reaction.

....

b Write the balanced chemical (symbol) equation for this reaction, including state symbols.

....

10 Write word equations for the following reactions:

a $Zn + CuSO_4 \rightarrow ZnSO_4 + Cu$

....

b $NH_4Cl + NaOH \rightarrow NH_3 + NaCl + H_2O$

....

c $4Fe + 3O_2 \rightarrow 2Fe_2O_3$

....

11 Balance the following symbol equations:

a .....Na + ...$Cl_2 \rightarrow$ .....NaCl   c .....Fe_2O_3 + ...CO $\rightarrow$ .....Fe + ...CO_2

b .....SO_2 + ...$O_2 \rightarrow$ .....SO_3 d .....PbO + ... C $\rightarrow$ .....Pb + ...CO_2

TIP
When balancing symbol equations, do not change any of the formulae of the substances involved. Always balance by putting whole numbers in front of the formulae.

Practice

12 Table 4.1 shows the valencies and formulae of some common ions.

		Valency		
		1	**2**	**3**
Positive ions (cations)	metals	sodium (Na^+) potassium (K^+) silver (Ag^+)	magnesium (Mg^{2+}) copper (Cu^{2+}) zinc (Zn^{2+}) iron (Fe^{2+})	aluminium (Al^{3+}) iron (Fe^{3+}) chromium (Cr^{3+})
	compound ions	ammonium (NH_4^+)		
Negative ions (anions)	non-metals	choride (Cl^-) bromide (Br^-) iodide (I^-)	oxide (O^{2-}) sulphide (S^{2-})	nitride (N^{3-})
	compound ions	nitrate (NO_3^-) hydroxide (OH^-)	carbonate (CO_3^{2-}) sulfate (SO_4^{2-})	phosphate (PO_4^{3-})

Table 4.1: Valencies and formulae of some common ions.

Use the information in the table to work out the formulae of the following ionic compounds:

a Copper oxide ....

b Sodium carbonate ....

c Zinc sulfate ....

d Silver nitrate ....

e Ammonium sulfate ....

f Potassium phosphate ....

g Iron(III) hydroxide ....

h Chromium(III) chloride ....

13 Use the information in Table 4.1 and your answers in **10** to give the ratio of the different atoms in the following compounds.

   a   Copper oxide Cu : O ....

   b   Iron(III) hydroxide Fe : O : H ....

   c   Ammonium sulfate N : H : S : O ....

14 Figure 4.3 is a representation of the structure of an ionic oxide.

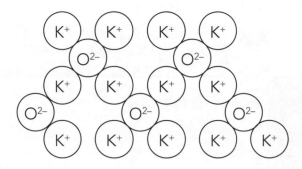

Figure 4.3: Structure of an ionic oxide.

   a   What is the ratio of K⁺ ions to O²⁻ ions? ....

   b   What is the formula of this compound? ....

> **TIP**
>
> When writing a formula of an ionic compound from a diagram of the structure, make sure you write the simplest ratio of the ions present.

Challenge

15 Figure 4.4 shows the structure of common salt.

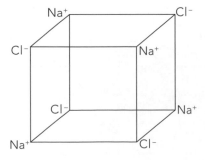

Figure 4.4: Structure of common salt.

a   Extend the structure in Figure 4.4 to the right by adding four more ions.

b   Complete Figure 4.5a and b for the ions in the structure to show their electronic configuration. Draw in any missing electron shells, showing clearly the origin of the electrons involved.

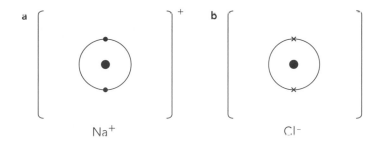

Figure 4.5: The electronic configuration of **a:** a sodium ion and **b:** a chloride ion.

16   Convert these equations into ionic equations:

a $Cl_2(aq) + 2KBr(aq) \rightarrow 2KCl(aq) + Br_2(aq)$

....

b $Mg(s) + 2HCl(aq) \rightarrow MgCl_2(aq) + H_2(g)$

....

c $FeCl_2(aq) + 2NaOH(aq) \rightarrow Fe(OH)_2(s) + 2NaCl(aq)$

....

d $ZnCl_2(aq) + Mg(s) \rightarrow MgCl_2(aq) + Zn(s)$

....

> Molecular masses and chemical reactions

KEY WORDS

relative atomic mass (A_r): the average mass of naturally occurring atoms of an element on a scale where an atom of carbon-12 has a mass of 12 exactly

relative formula mass (M_r): the sum of all the relative atomic masses of the atoms present in a 'formula unit' of a substance

relative molecular mass (M_r): the sum of all the relative atomic masses of the atoms present in a molecule

Exercise 4.3

IN THIS EXERCISE YOU WILL:

- use relative atomic mass to calculate the relative molecular or formula masses of compounds

- understand how relative molecular masses can be used to calculate the proportions of reactants and products

- develop your skills in processing and interpreting results from practical work

- show how experimental data can be used to find the proportions of reactants and products.

Focus

17 Complete Figure 4.6 by filling in the blanks.

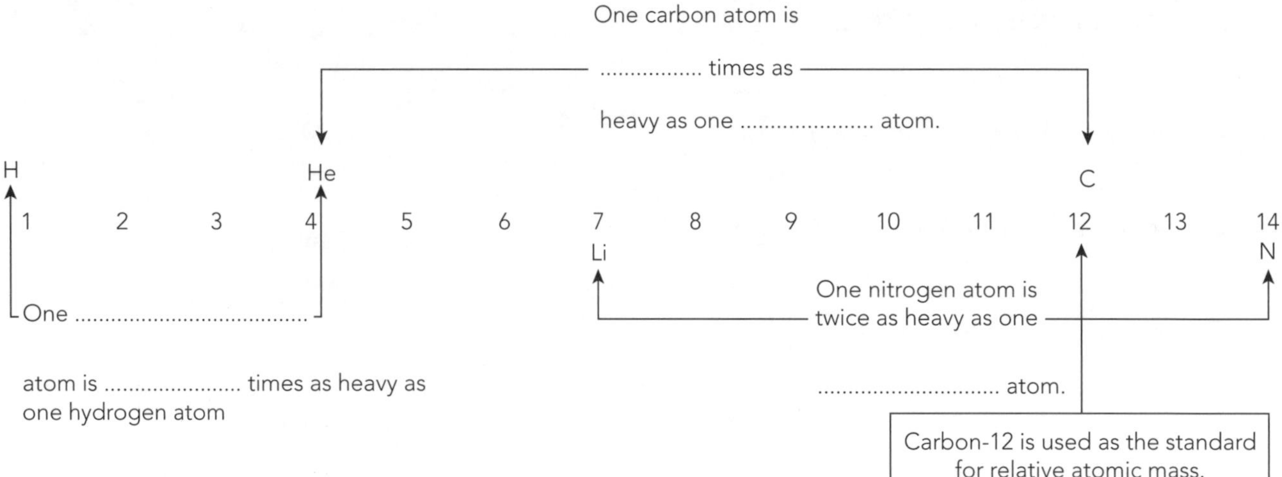

One carbon atom is

.... times as

heavy as one .... atom.

H			He								C		
1	2	3	4	5	6	7	8	9	10	11	12	13	14
						Li							N

One .... atom is .... times as heavy as one hydrogen atom

One nitrogen atom is twice as heavy as one .... atom.

Carbon-12 is used as the standard for relative atomic mass.

Figure 4.6: Relative atomic mass.

18 Zinc metal is extracted from its oxide. In the industrial extraction process, 5 tonnes of zinc oxide are needed to produce 4 tonnes of zinc. Calculate the mass of zinc, in tonnes, that is produced from 20 tonnes of zinc oxide.

....

19 When ammonia burns in oxygen, the following reaction takes place. The masses reacting are given along with the mass of nitrogen formed:

$$4NH_3 + 3O_2 \rightarrow 2N_2 + 6H_2O$$

68 g   96 g   56 g

a What mass of water is formed in this reaction? ....

....

b What mass of water is formed if 17 g of ammonia are burnt? ....

....

Practice

20   Complete Table 4.2 of the relative molecular (or formula) masses for a range of different substances.

(Relative atomic masses: O = 16, H = 1, C = 12, N = 14, Ca = 40, Mg = 24)

Molecule	Chemical formula	Number of atoms or ions involved	Relative molecular (or formula) mass
Oxygen	O_2	2O	$2 \times 16 = 32$
Carbon dioxide	....	1C and 2O	$1 \times 12 + 2 \times 16 =$ ....
....	H_2O	2H and 1O	.... = ...
Ammonia	....	1N and 3H	.... = ...
Calcium carbonate	....	$1Ca^{2+}$ and $1CO_3{}^{2-}$	.... + ... + $3 \times 16 = 100$
....	MgO	$1Mg^{2+}$ and $1O^{2-}$	$1 \times 24 + 1 \times 16 =$ ....
Ammonium nitrate	NH_4NO_3	$1NH_4{}^+$ and	$2 \times 14 +$ .... + ... = 80
Propanol	C_3H_7OH	3C, ... and	$3 \times 12 + 8 \times 1 +$ .... = ...

Table 4.2: Some relative molecular (or formula) masses.

Challenge

21   Magnesium oxide is made when magnesium is burnt in air. How does the mass of magnesium oxide made depend on the mass of magnesium burnt? The practical method is as follows.

Method

- Weigh an empty crucible and lid.

- Roll some magnesium ribbon around a pencil, place it in the crucible and re-weigh (not forgetting the lid).

- Place the crucible in a pipeclay triangle sitting safely on a tripod. (The lid should be on the crucible.)
- Heat the crucible and contents strongly (Figure 4.7), occasionally lifting the lid to allow more air in.

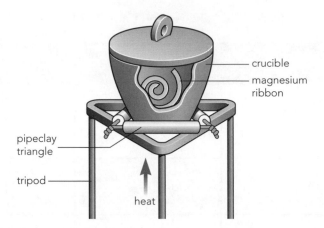

Figure 4.7: Heating magnesium ribbon.

- When the reaction has eased, take off the lid.
- Heat strongly for another three minutes.
- Let the crucible cool down and then weigh it.
- Repeat the heating until the mass is constant.

Results

Table 4.3 shows a set of class results calculated from the weights each student group obtained using this method.

Mass of magnesium / g	0.06	0.05	0.04	0.18	0.16	0.10	0.11	0.14	0.15	0.14	0.08	0.10	0.13
Mass of magnesium oxide / g	0.10	0.08	0.06	0.28	0.25	0.15	0.15	0.21	0.24	0.23	0.13	0.17	0.21

Table 4.3: Results for burning magnesium in air.

a   Use these results to plot a graph on the grid provided, relating the mass of magnesium oxide made to the mass of magnesium used. Remember there is one point on this graph that you can be certain of – think carefully what that point should be. Include it on your graph. Then answer the questions based on these results.

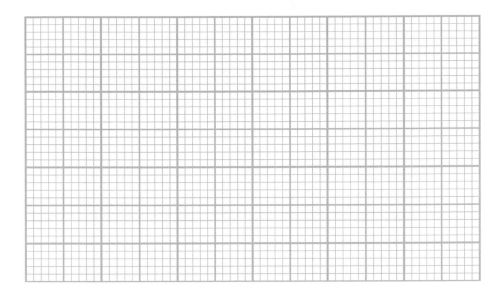

b   How does the mass of magnesium oxide depend on the starting mass of magnesium?

....

c   Use the graph to work out the mass of magnesium oxide that you would get from 0.12 g of magnesium (show the lines you use for this on your graph). ....g

d   What mass of oxygen combines with 0.12 g of magnesium? ....g

e   What mass of oxygen combines with 24 g of magnesium? ....g

f   If you were provided with 3.5 g of magnesium and heated it in a crucible, how much magnesium oxide would be formed? (Assume that the reaction goes to completion.)

....

....

g   Would magnesium oxide be the only product formed in this reaction?
Suggest another possible product and give the formula of that product.

....

SELF-ASSESSMENT

Drawing graphs from experimental data is an important aspect of practical work. Was your answer for the mass of magnesium oxide in question **21c** correct? Did you present the results of the experiment clearly so that they could be properly interpreted? Did you pay sufficient attention to plotting the points on a suitable scale and drawing the line of best fit carefully? You can use the general principles in the checklist in Chapter 1 to help you assess how well you have drawn the graph.

Chapter 5

Chemical calculations

> Chemical composition, reactions and purity

KEY WORDS

mass concentration: the measure of the concentration of a solution in terms of the mass of the solute, in grams, dissolved per cubic decimetre of solution (g/dm^3)

molar concentration: the measure of the concentration of a solution in terms of the number of moles of the solute dissolved per cubic decimetre of solution (mol/dm^3)

mole: the measure of amount of substance in chemistry; 1 mole of a substance has a mass equal to its relative formula mass in grams – that amount of substance contains 6.02×10^{23} (the Avogadro constant) atoms, molecules or formula units depending on the substance considered

percentage composition: the percentage by mass of each element in a compound

percentage purity: a measure of the purity of the product from a reaction carried out experimentally:

$$\text{percentage purity} = \frac{\text{mass of pure product}}{\text{mass of impure product}} \times 100$$

percentage yield: a measure of the actual yield of a reaction when carried out experimentally compared to the theoretical yield calculated from the equation:

$$\text{percentage yield} = \frac{\text{actual yield}}{\text{predicted yield}} \times 100$$

titration: a method of quantitative analysis using solutions: one solution is slowly added to a known volume of another solution using a burette until an end-point is reached

Exercise 5.1

IN THIS EXERCISE YOU WILL:

> calculate the percentage composition of a compound from the formula mass of a compound

> calculate the empirical formula and relate it to the molecular formula of a compound.

Focus

1   Complete the diagram shown in Figure 5.1 to work out the formula mass of the iron oxide in the ore magnetite. (A_r: Fe = 56, O = 16.) Then use the following steps to work out the percentage by mass of iron in this ore.

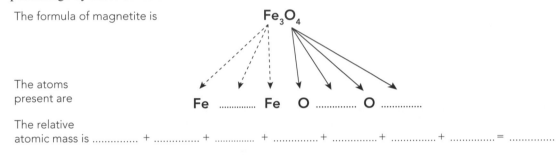

The formula of magnetite is Fe_3O_4

The atoms present are   Fe .... Fe   O .... O ....

The relative atomic mass is .... + ... + ... + ... + ... + ... + ... = ...

Figure 5.1: Chemical formula of magnetite, a form of iron oxide.

- The relative formula mass of the iron oxide (Fe_3O_4) = ...
- In this formula, there are .... atoms of iron, Fe.
- The relative mass of .... Fe = ...
- This means that in ....g of Fe_3O_4 there are ....g of iron.
- So 1 g of Fe_3O_4 contains ....g of iron.
- So 100 g of Fe_3O_4 contains ....g of iron.
- In other words, the percentage (%) of iron in Fe_3O_4 = ...%.

2   Oxalic acid is an organic acid present in rhubarb and some other vegetables. The composition by mass of oxalic acid is given below, and it has an M_r of 90.

carbon = 26.7%   hydrogen = 2.2%   oxygen = 71.1%

a   What is the empirical formula of oxalic acid?

....

....

....

....

b Calculate the molecular formula of the acid. ....

....

3 A volatile arsenic compound containing arsenic, carbon and hydrogen has the following composition by mass:

arsenic = 62.5%   carbon = 30.0%   hydrogen = 7.5%

Calculate the empirical formula of this compound.

....

....

....

> **TIP**
>
> Always show your working in calculations. It makes it easier to check whether you have made an error at some stage, and you can then correct it.

Exercise 5.2

> **IN THIS EXERCISE YOU WILL:**
>
> > apply the concept of the mole to industrial-scale reacting amounts
>
> > calculate the percentage yield of a chemical process.

Practice

In the laboratory, we are used to working with grams of material and our calculations are usually framed on that basis. However, an industrial chemist is often used to working on a significantly larger scale and looking to produce tonnes of product.

4 In this context, it is useful to know that the reacting proportions determined by the equation for the reaction can be readily scaled up to provide useful data at an industrial level.

> **TIP**
>
> Remember that one tonne (a metric ton) = 1000 kilograms.

a What mass of iron(III) oxide is needed to produce 100 g of iron, in the blast furnace? Complete the following sentence using your calculated figures. (A_r: C = 12; O = 16; Fe = 56)

The equation for the reaction is:

$Fe_2O_3(s) + 3CO(g) \rightarrow 2Fe(s) + 3CO_2(g)$

....

....

....

100 g of iron is .... moles of Fe, so .... moles of Fe_2O_3 are

needed for the reaction, or ....g of iron(III) oxide.

b Using your calculated value for how much iron(III) oxide (hematite) is needed to produce 100 g of iron, state how much hematite is needed to produce 50 tonnes of iron.

....

....

c Realistically, industrial processes and laboratory experiments do not produce perfect yields. In a particular blast furnace, 100 tonnes of hematite gave 7 tonnes of iron. Calculate the percentage yield of the process.

....

....

....

....

5 Another large-scale industrial process is the production of quicklime (calcium oxide, CaO) from limestone by heating in a lime kiln.

a What is the equation for the thermal decomposition of limestone?

....

b Using your equation, calculate how many tonnes of quicklime (calcium oxide, CaO) would be produced from 1 tonne of limestone. (A_r: Ca = 40)

....

....

....

c   In one production run, 2.5 tonnes of limestone were found to give 1.12 tonnes of quicklime. What is the percentage yield for this process? Give one reason why this yield is not 100%.

....

....

....

....

Exercise 5.3

IN THIS EXERCISE YOU WILL:

> apply the concept of the mole to calculations on the concentration of solutions

> consider how the results of titration experiments are calculated

> find the percentage yield of a reaction using a titration.

Challenge

6   Citric acid is an organic acid which is a white solid at room temperature. It dissolves readily in water.

The purity of a sample of the acid was tested by the following method.

Step 1: A sample of 0.48 g citric acid was dissolved in 50 cm³ of distilled water.

Step 2: Drops of thymolphthalein indicator were added.

Step 3: The solution was then titrated with a solution of sodium hydroxide (0.50 mol/dm³).

a Complete the labels for the pieces of apparatus used and give the colour of the solution before titration (Figure 5.2).

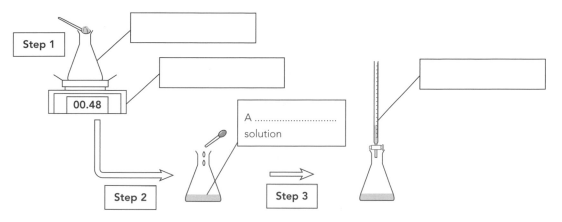

Figure 5.2: Experimental method for the titration of citric acid.

b These were the burette readings from the titration. Complete Table 5.1 by filling in the missing value (P).

Final burette reading / cm³	14.60
First burette reading / cm³	0.20
Volume of NaOH(aq) added / cm³	.... (P)

Table 5.1: Burette readings.

c Calculate the purity of the citric acid by following the stages outlined here.

Stage 1: Calculate the number of moles of alkali solution reacted in the titration.

• P cm³ of NaOH(aq) containing 0.50 moles in 1000 cm³ were used.

• Number of moles NaOH used $= \dfrac{0.50}{1000} \times P = Q = $ .... moles.

Stage 2: Calculate the number of moles of citric acid in the sample.

• Note that one mole of citric acid reacts with three moles of sodium hydroxide.

• Then number of moles of citric acid in sample $= \dfrac{Q}{3} = R = $ .... moles.

Stage 3: Calculate the mass of citric acid in the sample and therefore the percentage purity.

• Relative formula mass of citric acid (M_r of $C_6H_8O_7$) = ... (A_r: C = 12, H = 1, O = 16)

• Mass of citric acid in sample $= R \times M_r = S = $ .... g.

• Percentage purity of sample $= \dfrac{S}{0.48} = $ .... %.

d How could the sample of citric acid be purified further?

....

....

7 Hydrated crystals of copper(II) sulfate-5-water were prepared by the following reactions:

$CuO(s) + H_2SO_4(aq) \rightarrow CuSO_4(aq) + H_2O(l)$

$CuSO_4(aq) + 5H_2O(l) \rightarrow CuSO_4 \cdot 5H_2O(s)$

In an experiment, 25 cm³ of 2 mol/dm³ sulfuric acid was neutralised with an excess of copper(II) oxide. The yield of crystals, $CuSO_4 \cdot 5H_2O$, was 7.3 g.

Complete the following to calculate the percentage yield.

- Number of moles of H_2SO_4 in 25 cm³ of 2 mol/dm³ solution =

  ....

- Maximum number of moles of $CuSO_4 \cdot 5H_2O$ that could be formed =

  ....

- Maximum mass of crystals, $CuSO_4 \cdot 5H_2O$, that could be formed =

  ....

  (The mass of one mole of $CuSO_4 \cdot 5H_2O$ is 250 g.)

- Percentage yield = ... %

> Calculations on the mole

KEY WORDS

molar gas volume: 1 mole of any gas has the same volume under the same conditions of temperature and pressure (24 dm³ at r.t.p.)

r.t.p.: room temperature and pressure: the standard values are 25 °C/298 K and 101.3 kPa/1 atmosphere pressure

Exercise 5.4

IN THIS EXERCISE YOU WILL:

> investigate the conversion of the mass of a substance into moles

> use the molar concentration of a solution to calculate the number of moles in a particular volume of that solution

> use calculation triangles as a memory aid in calculations on the mole.

Focus

8 The mathematical equation that relates the mass of a substance (in g) to the number of moles present is:

$$\text{number of moles} = \frac{\text{mass}}{\text{molar mass}}$$

If two of these values are known, then the third can be calculated by rearranging this equation. A calculation triangle can be set up which helps you check that you have rearranged the equation correctly.

Fill in the calculation triangle (Figure 5.3) for changing between masses and moles. Then complete Table 5.2. (A_r: H = 1, C = 12, N = 14, O = 16, Mg = 24, S = 32, Cl = 35.5, Ca = 40, Cu = 64)

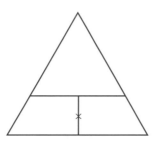

Figure 5.3: Calculation triangle for converting mass to moles.

Substance	A_r or M_r	Number of moles	Mass / g
Cu			128.0
Mg		0.5	
Cl_2			35.5
H_2			4.0
S_8		2.0	
O_3			1.6
H_2SO_4		2.5	
CO_2		0.4	
NH_3			25.5
$CaCO_3$			100.0
$MgSO_4 \cdot 7H_2O$			82.0

Table 5.2: Calculations on moles and mass of substance.

9 a Using your answer from the first row of Table 5.2, calculate the number of atoms present in 128 g of copper.

....

....

b Again referring to your answer in Table 5.2, how many hydrogen atoms are present in 4 g of hydrogen gas?

....

....

10 The mole can also be used as a measure of the concentration of a solution; the molar concentration having the units mol/dm^3. The number of moles in a given solution can be calculated using the mathematical equation:

number of moles in solution = molar concentration × volume of solution (in dm^3)

This equation can also be rearranged to find an unknown value if the other two values are known. As in question **8**, a calculation triangle can be set up so you can check that your rearrangement of the equation is correct.

Fill in the calculation triangle (Figure 5.4), relating moles of solute to volume and concentration. Then complete Table 5.3.

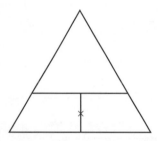

Figure 5.4: Calculation triangle relating moles of solute and concentration.

Solute	Volume of solution	Molar concentration of solution / mol per dm³	Moles of solute present
Sodium chloride	1 dm³	0.5	
Hydrochloric acid	500 cm³	0.5	
Sodium hydroxide	2 dm³		1.00
Sulfuric acid	250 cm³		0.50
Sodium thiosulfate		2.0	0.40
Copper(II) sulfate		0.1	0.75

Table 5.3: Calculations of moles in solution.

TIP

Mole calculations involving concentrations of solution are easier if you change cm^3 to dm^3 and then use these values in the formula. Remember you have a check on the formula from the 'triangle': $concentration = \dfrac{number\ of\ moles}{volume\ of\ solution\ in\ dm^3}$

PEER ASSESSMENT

Together with a partner, check your answers in these tables in this exercise and use them to challenge and test each other with different combinations of values. The use of calculation triangles is one strategy to help you understand the relationships involved in molar calculations. Discuss the use of calculation triangles with your partner and ask your partner to give an explanation of how to use these triangles. Was your partner's explanation correct? What other strategies could you think of?

Exercise 5.5

IN THIS EXERCISE YOU WILL:

> convert the mass of a substance into moles

> consider the relationship between volume and the number of moles of a gas.

Practice

From the chemical equation for the reaction and using the relative formula masses together with the molar gas volume, it is possible to predict the amounts of magnesium sulfate and hydrogen that are produced when 24 g of magnesium are reacted with excess sulfuric acid.

$$Mg \quad + \quad H_2SO_4 \quad \rightarrow \quad MgSO_4 \quad + \quad H_2$$

$$24\,g \qquad\qquad excess \qquad\qquad 120\,g \qquad\qquad 24\,000\,cm^3$$

This relationship between the mass of magnesium used and the volume of gas produced can be used to find the mass of a short piece of magnesium ribbon indirectly.

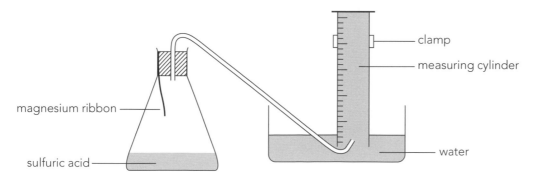

Figure 5.5: Experimental setup to find the mass of a piece of magnesium ribbon.

The experimental instructions were as follows:

- Wear safety goggles for eye protection.

- Set up the apparatus as shown in Figure 5.5, with 25 cm³ of sulfuric acid in the flask.

- Make sure the measuring cylinder is completely full of water.

- Carefully measure 5 cm of magnesium ribbon and use the flask stopper to grip the ribbon as shown.

- Ease the stopper up to release the ribbon and immediately replace the stopper.

- When no further bubbles rise into the measuring cylinder, record the volume of gas collected.

- Repeat the experiment twice more using 5 cm of magnesium ribbon and fresh sulfuric acid each time.

- Find the mean average volume of hydrogen produced.

A student obtained the results shown in Table 5.4 when measuring the volume of hydrogen produced.

Experiment number	Volume of hydrogen collected / cm³
1	85
2	79
3	82
Mean average	....

Table 5.4: Experimental results: volume of hydrogen produced.

11 Fill in the mean average of the results obtained. Can you think of possible reasons why the three results are not the same?

....

....

....

12 You know that 24 g of magnesium will produce 24 000 cm³ of hydrogen at r.t.p. What mass of magnesium would be needed to produce your volume of hydrogen?

....

....

Your answer here is the mass of 5 cm of magnesium ribbon. The weight is too low to weigh easily on a balance but you could weigh a longer length and use that to check your answer.

13 What mass of magnesium sulfate would you expect 5 cm of magnesium ribbon to produce?

....

....

14 Plan an experiment to check whether your prediction in question **13** is correct.

....

....

....

....

....

....

....

Exercise 5.6

IN THIS EXERCISE YOU WILL:

> deduce the formula of a compound from data on reacting gas volumes.

Challenge

Experiments show that volumes of gases react together in a ratio that can be predicted from the chemical equation for a reaction.

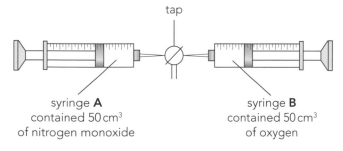

tap

syringe **A**
contained 50 cm³
of nitrogen monoxide

syringe **B**
contained 50 cm³
of oxygen

Figure 5.6: Syringe apparatus for a gas experiment.

Under the conditions used here, nitrogen monoxide (NO) reacts with oxygen (O_2) to form one product that is a brown gas. In an experiment, 5 cm³ portions of oxygen were pushed from syringe B into syringe A (Figure 5.6).

After each addition, the tap was closed, the gases were cooled, and then the total volume of gases remaining was measured. The results are shown in Figure 5.7.

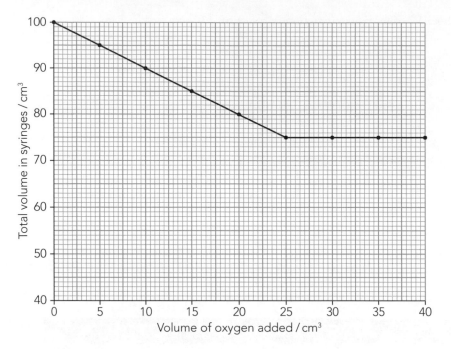

Figure 5.7: Graph of experimental results.

15 What is the total volume of gases when the reaction is complete?

....

16 What volume of oxygen reacts with 50 cm³ of nitrogen monoxide?

....

17 What is the volume of the brown gas formed?

....

18 Complete the following to work out the formula of the brown gas:

.... NO   + O_2 →   ....

    50 cm³   .....cm³   ..... cm³

> Chapter 6
Electrochemistry

> Electrical conductivity and the nature of electrolysis

KEY WORDS

anode: the electrode in any type of cell at which oxidation (the loss of electrons) takes place – in electrolysis it is the positive electrode

cathode: the electrode in any type of cell at which reduction (the gain of electrons) takes place; in electrolysis it is the negative electrode

electrodes: the points where the electric current enters or leaves a battery or electrolytic cell

electrolysis: the breakdown of an ionic compound, molten or in aqueous solution, by the use of electricity

electrolyte: an ionic compound that will conduct electricity when it is molten or dissolved in water; electrolytes will not conduct electricity when solid

electrolytic cell: a cell consisting of an electrolyte and two electrodes (anode and cathode) connected to an external DC power source where positive and negative ions in the electrolyte are separated and discharged

fuel cell: a device for continuously converting chemical energy into electrical energy using a combustion reaction; a hydrogen fuel cell uses the reaction between hydrogen and oxygen

Exercise 6.1

IN THIS EXERCISE YOU WILL:

- describe how metals are electrical conductors and non-metallic materials are non-conducting insulators

- investigate the process of electrolysis

- learn how to describe the electrode products of electrolysis.

Focus

1   Figure 6.1 shows an electrolytic cell that could be used to test whether a liquid substance or aqueous solution conducts electricity by electrolysis.

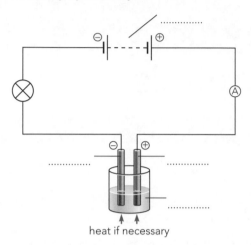

heat if necessary

Figure 6.1: Electrolytic cell for testing the electrical conductivity of a liquid or solution. Heat can be supplied if necessary.

a   Complete Figure 6.1 by labelling the electrolyte, the anode, the cathode and the power supply.

b   Name two substances that are often used as inert electrodes in such an electrolytic cell.

....

c   Complete the following statements about electrical conductivity and electrolysis by linking the phrases A to D on the left with phrases 1 to 4 on the right.

A Sulfur does not conduct electricity …	1 … because the ions present are in fixed positions in the structure and not free to move.
B Solid lead(II) bromide does not conduct electricity …	2 … because there are free delocalised electrons in the structure that are free to move.
C Metallic elements and alloys conduct electricity …	3 … because none of the electrons in the structure are free to move.
D Molten lead(II) bromide conducts electricity …	4 … because the ions present in the molten liquid are free to move.

2   Crystals of ionic compounds do not conduct electricity. However, when the crystals are melted and the molten liquid placed in an electrolytic cell, a current will flow. A chemical reaction takes place in which the ionic salt is decomposed into its elements.

Table 6.1 shows the electrolysis of several different molten binary compounds. Complete the table by filling in the electrode products following electrolysis. Complete the final column of the table with observations of the product given off at the anode.

Molten electrolyte	Product at anode (+)	Product at cathode (−)	Observations of product at anode
Lead(II) iodide			
Magnesium chloride			
Zinc bromide			
Calcium oxide			

Table 6.1: The electrolysis of molten ionic compounds.

> **TIP**
>
> During electrolysis, metals or hydrogen are formed at the cathode and non-metals (other than hydrogen) are formed at the anode.

Exercise 6.2

IN THIS EXERCISE YOU WILL:

- learn how, in electrolysis, the positive electrode is known as the anode, and the negative electrode is the cathode

- describe the terms anion (positive ion) and cation (negative ion) in relation to the direction an ion moves during electrolysis.

Practice

3 A student set up an experiment like this to show the movement of ions in solution (Figure 6.2). The filter paper is damp, and a small crystal of the solid being studied is placed in the centre as shown.

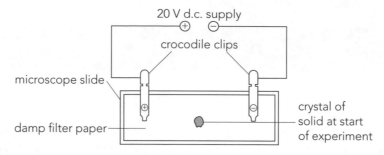

Figure 6.2: Experiment on the movement of ions in an electric field.

The results are shown in Table 6.2.

Substance	Colour of crystals	Changes seen on the filter paper
Potassium chromate, K_2CrO_4	yellow	yellow colour moves towards positive
Potassium sulfate, K_2SO_4	white	no colours seen
Copper sulfate, $CuSO_4$	blue	blue colour moves towards negative

Table 6.2: Results from an experiment on the movement of ions in an electric field.

a Which of these ions is yellow? Circle the correct answer.

chromate   copper   potassium   sulfate

b Explain why the yellow colour moves towards the positive terminal in the potassium chromate experiment.

....

....

c List the anions and cations involved in this experiment, together with their formulae.

Anions:

....

Cations:

....

d Suggest and explain what will happen if this experiment is repeated with copper chromate.

....

....

....

....

PEER ASSESSMENT

Discuss your answers to question **3d** with a partner. What is the difference between the command words 'suggest' and 'explain'? Have you suggested what will happen and explained why in your answer?

4 Using the words provided, complete the following passages; some words may be used more than once.

> **anode   cathode   current   electrodes   electrolyte   hydrogen   hydroxide**
>
> **lose   molecules   molten   positive   solution**

During electrolysis, ionic compounds are decomposed by the passage of an electric current.

For this to happen, the compound must be either .... or in ....

in water. Electrolysis can occur when an electric .... passes through a molten

.... The two rods dipping into the electrolyte are called the ....

In this situation, metals are deposited at the .... and non-metals are formed at

the ....

When the ionic compound is dissolved in water, the electrolysis can be more complex.

Generally, during electrolysis, ... ions move towards the .... and

negative ions move towards the .... At the negative electrode (cathode) the metal

or .... ions gain electrons and form metal atoms or hydrogen ....

At the positive electrode (anode) non-metals are formed as their ions or .... ions

from the water lose electrons.

Exercise 6.3

IN THIS EXERCISE YOU WILL:

- review the basic features of electrolysis

> investigate how a hydrogen–oxygen fuel cell can be used to power vehicles

> describe the products of electrolysis of dilute and concentrated halide solutions

> state the type of reaction taking place at the electrodes during electrolysis and construct electrode half-equations.

Challenge

5   Table 6.3 lists the results of the electrolysis of a number of aqueous solutions using inert electrodes. Use the information in the top part of the table to complete the blank spaces. The solutions were all electrolysed under exactly the same conditions.

Solution (electrolyte)	Gas given off at the anode	Gas given off or metal deposited at the cathode	Substance left in solution at the end of electrolysis
Copper(II) sulfate	oxygen	copper	sulfuric acid
Sodium sulfate	oxygen	hydrogen	sodium sulfate
Concentrated sodium chloride	chlorine	hydrogen	sodium hydroxide
Silver nitrate	oxygen	silver	nitric acid
Concentrated potassium bromide		hydrogen	
Copper(II) nitrate		copper	nitric acid
Silver sulfate	oxygen		
Sodium nitrate		hydrogen	sodium nitrate

Table 6.3: The electrolysis of aqueous solutions using inert electrodes.

6 Figure 6.3 shows the basic structure of a hydrogen fuel cell.

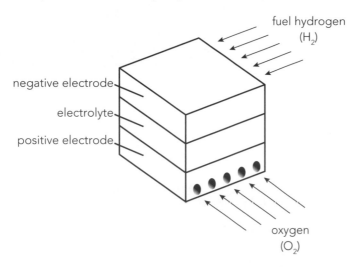

Figure 6.3: The structure of a hydrogen fuel cell.

a Hydrogen gas enters the cell at the negative electrode and is converted into hydrogen (H^+) ions. Write the ionic half-equation for this electrode reaction.

....

b In a hydrogen fuel cell with an acidic electrolyte, oxygen enters the cell and reacts with the hydrogen ions in the electrolyte to produce water. Balance the electrode half-equation for this reaction.

$O_2(g) + \ldots\ldots H^+(aq) + \ldots\ldots e^- \rightarrow \ldots\ldots H_2O(l)$

c Add the two half-equations from **a** and **b** together to give the overall reaction.

....

> **TIP**
>
> Half-equations are ionic equations that show the individual reactions at the anode (oxidation) and cathode (reduction) in an electrochemical cell. Half-equations are balanced when each side is neutral.

d Give two advantages of using hydrogen–oxygen fuel cells to power vehicles.

....

....

e Suggest two practical problems that will need to be overcome to fully use hydrogen–oxygen fuel cells for a carbon-neutral road transport system.

....

....

> Electrolysis using copper salts

KEY WORD

electroplating: a process of electrolysis in which a metal object is coated (plated) with a layer of another metal

Exercise 6.4

IN THIS EXERCISE YOU WILL:

- describe how electrolysis can be used to electroplate a metal object

> investigate the electrolysis of copper(II) chloride solution using carbon electrodes

> learn how changing the nature of the electrodes alters the products formed during electrolysis.

Focus

A metal jug can be electroplated with copper as shown in Figure 6.4.

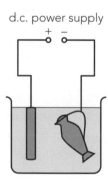

d.c. power supply
+ −

Figure 6.4: Electroplating an object with copper.

7 **a** On Figure 6.4 label the anode A, the cathode C and the electrolyte E.

b What metal must be used for the anode? ....

c Name a salt that could be used in solution as the electrolyte. ....

d What is seen to happen to the anode as the electroplating takes place?

....

e What are the two main reasons for electroplating an object?

....

....

> # Practice

8 Copper(II) chloride can be decomposed to its elements by electrolysis of a solution of the salt. A simple cell (Figure 6.5) can be set up so that the chlorine gas can be collected.

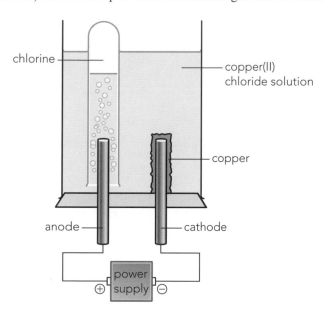

Figure 6.5: Electrolysis of copper(II) chloride solution.

a Write the word and balanced symbol equations for the overall reaction taking place during this electrolysis.

....

....

b How would you test the gas collected at the anode to show that it was chlorine?

....

c Is the decomposition of copper(II) chloride exothermic or endothermic? What type of energy is involved in this reaction?

....

....

Challenge

9 Figure 6.6 shows the electrolytic cell used in the electrolysis of copper(II) sulfate solution using copper electrodes.

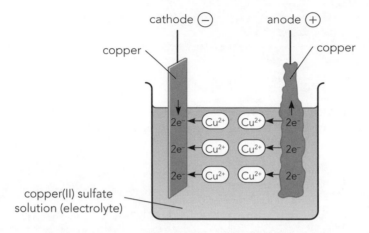

Figure 6.6: The electrolysis of copper(II) sulfate using copper electrodes.

a Use information from Figure 6.6 to write half-equations for the reactions taking place at the cathode and anode in this electrolysis.

i At the cathode:

....

ii At the anode:

....

b Predict the change in mass of the copper electrodes that could be detected if the electrolysis was carried out for a sufficient period of time.

i Change in mass of the cathode:

....

....

ii Change in mass of the anode:

....

....

c Explain why the colour of the copper(II) sulfate solution does not change during the electrolysis.

....

....

....

....

> Chapter 7

Chemical energetics

> Chemical and physical changes

KEY WORDS

chemical reaction (change): a change in which a new substance is formed

physical change: a change in the physical state of a substance or the physical nature of a situation that does not involve a change in the chemical substance(s) present

---

Exercise 7.1

IN THIS EXERCISE YOU WILL:

- identify physical and chemical changes and understand the differences between them
- use the criteria for identifying physical and chemical changes to classify different changes.

Focus

1   Using the words provided, complete the following paragraph. Words may be used once, more than once or not at all.

chemical   chemically   different to   physical   reverse   the same as

When a .... change takes place, the substance undergoing the change is

unchanged .... When a .... change takes place, the substance or

substances formed are .... the starting substance. Physical changes are easy to

.... so that we can easily go back to the starting substance. ....

changes are difficult to ...., so it is more difficult to form the starting

substance again.

Practice

2   For each of the following changes, identify it as either a chemical or physical change and give two reasons for your answer.

   a   Ice melting

   ....

   ....

   ....

   b   Magnesium burning in air

   ....

   ....

   ....

   c   Salt dissolving in water

   ....

   ....

   ....

Challenge

3   When zinc carbonate ($ZnCO_3$) is heated strongly, the following observations are made:
   • A colourless gas is given off which turns limewater cloudy.
   • A solid is left that was yellow when hot and white when cold.
   • When this cold solid was heated it turned yellow again.
   • This solid contained zinc and one other element.

   a   Complete the flowchart by naming the chemicals in the boxes and writing the correct labels on the arrows.

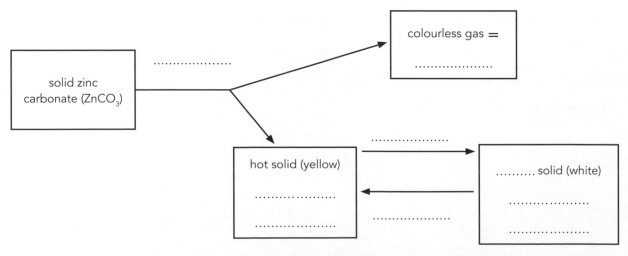

b   Write the balanced symbol equation for the change taking place when the zinc carbonate is heated strongly.

....

c   Is this a chemical or physical change? Explain your answer.

....

....

d   Why is this reaction a thermal decomposition reaction?

....

....

e   Identify a physical change shown in the flowchart and explain your choice.

....

....

> Exothermic and endothermic processes

KEY WORDS

endothermic change: a process or chemical reaction which takes in heat from the surroundings.
ΔH for an endothermic change has a positive value.

exothermic change: a process or chemical reaction in which heat energy is produced and released to the surroundings.
ΔH for an exothermic change has a negative value.

Exercise 7.2

IN THIS EXERCISE YOU WILL:

*   look at the properties of exothermic and endothermic changes

*   investigate the uses of these types of change

*   consider how a heat change in a chemical reaction can be followed practically

*   interpret the results from a practical investigation of a chemical reaction in which an energy change take place.

Focus

4   Draw lines between the two columns to show which statements are true for exothermic and
    endothermic reactions.

Type of reaction

Statement / Fact

The temperature decreases

Exothermic

Heat energy is given out to
the surroundings

The temperature increases

Endothermic

Combustion is an example of
this type of reaction

Heat energy is taken in from
the surroundings

Practice

5   The reaction between calcium oxide (slaked lime) and water can be used to heat up drinks like
    coffee and tea. When this reaction takes place, a great deal of heat is given off and the solid
    calcium oxide swells to occupy a greater volume.

    Figure 7.1 shows one way in which such a can may be constructed.

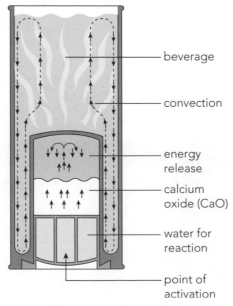

Figure 7.1: A self-heating drinks can.

a What term is used for a reaction that gives out heat to the external surroundings?

....

b What problem might arise because of the expansion of the solid when water is added?

....

c Look carefully at the diagram and suggest how this problem might be overcome.

....

d Write the word and balanced symbol equations for the reaction between calcium oxide and water to give calcium hydroxide.

....

....

Challenge

6 Reactions that absorb heat from the surroundings can be used where things need to be cooled down or kept cool. There are two types of cool pack (Figure 7.2):

- instant cool packs that contain a solid which dissolves endothermically in water that is kept separate from the solid in the package until needed

- cool packs that contain a gel which is cooled down in a freezer and which warms up slowly when removed. This type of cool pack can be reused.

Figure 7.2: Two types of cool pack.

Instant cool packs usually contain crystals of ammonium nitrate together with a plastic bag of water which is burst to activate the pack.

a Give one advantage and one disadvantage of this type of cool pack.

Advantage:

....

Disadvantage:

....

b   Cool packs can be used to keep vaccines and other medicines cool in hot climates. A temperature of 5 °C is usually required. You are asked to find the mass of ammonium nitrate that could be used with 10 cm³ of water to make a cool pack for medicines.

Briefly describe a plan for carrying out this investigation:

- Name the apparatus you would use.

- Give the variables you would control to make it a fair test (remember that everything should be the same except the thing you are testing).

- Describe how you would carry out the experiment and the measurements you would take.

- Explain how you would use your results to find the answer to the problem.

....

....

....

....

....

....

....

> **TIP**
>
> It would be very fortunate if you were to choose the mass of ammonium nitrate that would give a temperature change of exactly 5 °C. Think about how a graph would help you find the answer.

> Reaction pathway diagrams

> **KEY WORDS**
>
> **activation energy (E_a):** the minimum energy required to start a chemical reaction – for a reaction to take place the colliding particles must possess at least this amount of energy
>
> **enthalpy (H):** the thermal (heat) content of a system
>
> **enthalpy change (ΔH):** the heat change during the course of a reaction (also known as **heat of reaction**); can be either exothermic (a negative value) or endothermic (a positive value)
>
> **reaction pathway diagram (energy level diagram):** a diagram that shows the energy levels of the reactants and products in a chemical reaction and shows whether a reaction is exothermic or endothermic

Exercise 7.3

IN THIS EXERCISE YOU WILL:

- interpret reaction pathway diagrams for exothermic and endothermic reactions

> associate enthalpy changes with endothermic and exothermic reactions and give the correct sign for the enthalpy change for each type of reaction

> label reaction pathway diagrams to show the relationships between enthalpy changes due to a reaction and the activation energy for the reaction.

Focus

7   The energy changes involved in chemical reactions can be represented visually by reaction pathway (or energy level) diagrams. These diagrams show the relative stability of the reactants and products. The more stable a set of reactants or products, the lower their energy level.

The reaction pathway diagram for an exothermic reaction is different from that for an endothermic reaction.

a   Delete the incorrect words in the following paragraph. Use Figure 7.3 to help you.

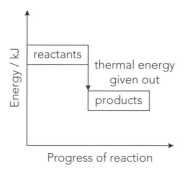

Figure 7.3: Reaction pathway diagram for an exothermic reaction.

In an exothermic reaction, the **reactants / products** have more thermal energy than the **reactants / products**. This means that **thermal energy / potential energy** is transferred **to / from** the surroundings and therefore the temperature of the surroundings **increases / decreases**.

TIP

When you measure the temperature of the reaction mixture, you measure the temperature of the surroundings not the reaction itself.

b   Delete the incorrect words in the following paragraph. Use Figure 7.4 to help you.

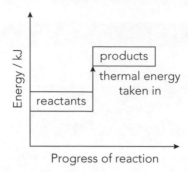

Figure 7.4: Reaction pathway diagram for an endothermic reaction.

In an endothermic reaction, the **reactants / products** have more thermal energy than the **reactants / products**. This means that energy is transferred **to / from** the surroundings and the temperature of the surroundings **increases / decreases**.

> Practice

8   The following equations show two chemical reactions along with the enthalpy change for each reaction.

$$CH_4(g) + O_2(g) \longrightarrow CO_2(g) + 2H_2O(l) \qquad \Delta H = -891 \, kJ/mol$$

$$CaCO_3(s) \xrightarrow{\text{heat}} CaO(s) + CO_2(g) \qquad \Delta H = +178 \, kJ/mol$$

Using this information, insert the correct reactants (e.g. $CH_4 + 2O_2$) and products (e.g. $CO_2 + 2H_2O$) in the incomplete reaction pathway diagrams in Figures 7.5 and 7.6. Write the symbols for the reactants in the left-hand boxes and the products in the right-hand boxes. Label the arrows with the correct value for the enthalpy change.

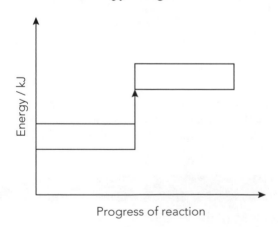

Figure 7.5: Reaction pathway diagram.

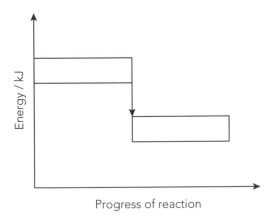

Figure 7.6: Reaction pathway diagram.

Challenge

9 Reaction pathway diagrams show how the energy changes during a reaction. Complete reaction pathway diagrams also include the activation energy (E_a). This is the energy required for the reaction to take place.

A complete reaction pathway diagram is shown in Figure 7.7.

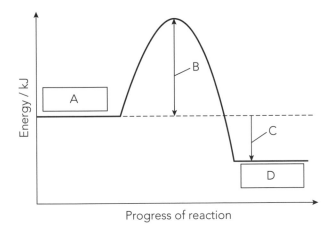

Figure 7.7: Reaction pathway diagram.

a Give the correct labels for A–D.

A ....

B ....

C ....

D ....

b The reaction between nitrogen and hydrogen to form ammonia is one of the most important of all chemical reactions. The equation for the reaction is shown below, along with information regarding the enthalpy change for the reaction and the activation energy (E_a).

$$N_2(g) + 3H_2 \rightarrow 2NH_3(g) \quad E_a = +2000\,\text{kJ/mol} \qquad \Delta H = -92\,\text{kJ/mol}$$

In the space provided, draw a reaction pathway diagram for this reaction.

- Draw and label the axes.

- Draw the reaction pathway expected for this reaction.

- Write the reactants and products in the correct places.

- Draw labelled lines to show the enthalpy change of the reaction and the activation energy, and give the correct values.

> Bond energies

IN THIS EXERCISE YOU WILL:

- identify the type and number of bonds present in covalent compounds

> identify the differences in ΔH when bonds are made and broken

> calculate the energies required to break these bonds

> calculate the energy given off when these bonds are made

> calculate the enthalpy change of reaction using the energy taken in by bond breaking and the energy given out when bonds are made.

Exercise 7.4

Focus

10 Using the words provided, complete the following paragraph. Note that not all the words should be used, and one word should be used twice.

> **broken   endothermic   exothermic   given out   kilogram**
>
> **kilojoules   made   mole   negative   positive   taken in**

The bond energy is the energy required to break one .... of covalent bonds.

The energy is measured in .... When bonds are .... energy

has to be added to the system and the sign for ΔH is .... When bonds are

.... energy is given out by the system and the sign for ΔH is ....

The enthalpy change for the reaction is the difference between the energy ....

when bonds are broken and the energy .... when bonds are ....

If the overall change in enthalpy is negative then the reaction is .... If it is

positive then the reaction is an .... one.

Practice

11 Table 7.1 shows the energy required to break one mole of different types of covalent bond.

Bond	Bond energy / kJ per mole
C–C	347
C–H	413
C=O	805
O=O	498
O–H	464

Table 7.1: The bond energies of some covalent bonds.

a   Identify from the table:

   i   the weakest bond ....

   ii   the strongest bond ....

b   i   Calculate the number of moles of O–H bonds in two moles of water.

        ....

   ii   Calculate the energy required to break all these bonds.

        ....

c   When methane (CH_4) reacts with oxygen (O=O), carbon dioxide (O=C=O) and water (H–O–H) are formed.

   The equation for the reaction is: $CH_4(g) + 2O_2(g) \rightarrow CO_2(g) + 2H_2O(l)$

   i   Identify and calculate the number of bonds broken in the reaction.

        ....

   ii   Identify and calculate the number of bonds made in the reaction.

        ....

Challenge

12 Propane burns in oxygen to form carbon dioxide and water.

   The equation for the reaction is: $C_3H_8(g) + 5O_2(g) \rightarrow 3CO_2(g) + 4H_2O(l)$

   a   Identify the type and number of bonds broken.

      ....

      ....

   b   Calculate the ΔH for bond breaking. Use the bond energies given in Table 7.1.

      ....

      ....

c   Identify the type and number of bonds made.

....

....

d   Calculate the ΔH for bond making. Use the bond energies given in Table 7.1.

....

....

e   Calculate the enthalpy change for the reaction.

....

....

f   Calculate how much energy is released when the following amounts of propane are burnt.
    (A_r: C = 12; H = 1)

   i   0.2 mol:

....

....

   ii   4 mol:

....

....

   iii 33 g:

....

....

PEER ASSESSMENT

Get together with a partner and compare your answers for questions **11–13** in this exercise.

- Have you both identified the correct types and numbers of bonds?

- Explain to your partner how you carried out the calculations and what you found easy or hard about them.

- Then listen to their account of how they did it.

> Chapter 8

Rates of reaction

> Factors affecting the rates of chemical reaction

KEY WORDS

reaction rate: a measure of how fast a reaction takes place

Exercise 8.1

IN THIS EXERCISE YOU WILL:

- investigate what is meant by surface area and predict its effects on the rate of a chemical reaction

- look at an experiment to investigate the effect of surface area on reaction rate

- analyse the data from the experiment and plot a graph of the results

- use the results to deduce the effect of changing surface area on reaction rate.

Focus

1   Figure 8.1 shows a large piece (A) of calcium carbonate (marble chips) and the same piece broken into smaller pieces (B).

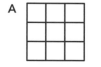

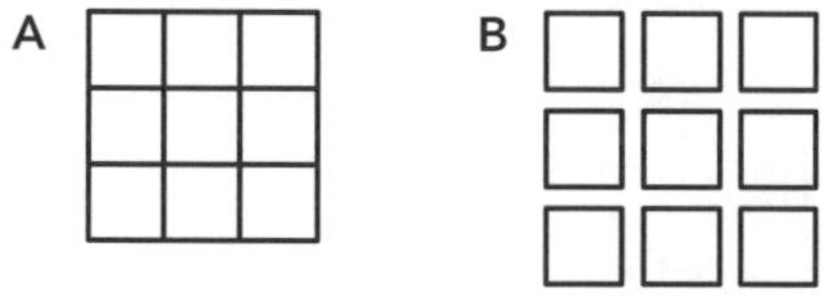

Figure 8.1: Calcium carbonate: a large piece (A) and broken into smaller pieces (B).

a   Using the diagram, explain which of A or B has the greater surface area.

....

....

b   When solid calcium carbonate (marble chips) reacts with hydrochloric acid, carbon dioxide, calcium chloride solution and water are formed.

Write the word equation for this reaction, including state symbols.

....

We can use this reaction to investigate the effect of changing the surface area on the rate of reaction. The carbon dioxide gas given off means that the mass of the reaction mixture changes. The apparatus used is shown in Figure 8.2.

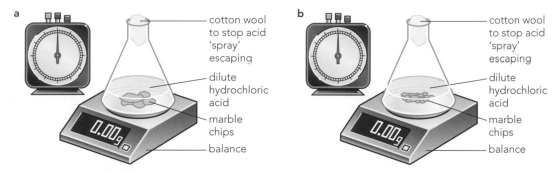

Figure 8.2: Experiment with **a:** large marble chips and acid and **b:** small marble chips and acid.

2   Does the mass measured on the balance increase or decrease in this reaction? Explain your answer.

....

....

Practice

3   In order to make the experiment give a clear result (a fair test), the only factor that is changed in the experiment shown in Figure 8.2 is the surface area of the calcium carbonate. Give four factors that must be kept constant (the same) in both experiments.

....

....

....

....

4   Choose one of these factors and explain its effect on the rate of reaction in terms of collision theory.

....

....

....

5 Using the words provided, complete the following paragraph. Note not all of the words should be used, and one word should be used twice.

collide   connect   inside   outside   react

In the reaction between calcium carbonate and hydrochloric acid, the acid particles can only

collide and .... with the calcium carbonate particles on the ....

of the pieces, the ones on the .... cannot react. In the smaller pieces, more of

the .... particles are exposed to the acid and the acid particles can therefore

.... with more calcium carbonate particles and more reactions take place.

Challenge

Flask A contains larger pieces of marble chips and Flask B contains smaller pieces.

The change in mass of the flasks was then recorded over time.

Readings on the digital balance were taken every 30 seconds. These are shown in Tables 8.1a and 8.1b.

For the large pieces of marble chips (flask A), readings (in grams) were:

Time / s	0	30	60	90	120	150	180	210
Mass / g	240.86	240.65	240.40	240.21	240.10	240.05	239.95	239.94
Loss in mass / g	0.00	0.21	0.46					
Time / s	240	270	300	330	360	390	420	450
Mass / g	239.90	239.88	239.87	239.86	239.86	239.86	239.86	239.86
Loss in mass / g								

Table 8.1 a: Experimental results – flask A.

For the small pieces of marble chips (flask B), readings (in grams) were:

Time / s	0	30	60	90	120	150	180	210
Mass / g	240.86	240.35	240.08	239.99	239.95	239.92	239.90	239.88
Loss in mass / g	0.00							
Time / s	240	270	300	330	360	390	420	450
Mass / g	239.87	239.86	239.86	239.86	239.86	239.86	239.86	239.86
Loss in mass / g								

Table 8.1 b: Experimental results – flask B.

6   a   Fill in the gaps in both of the tables by calculating the loss in mass at the different times. The first three have been done for you.

    b   Plot the two graphs for flasks A and B on the grid provided. Your graphs should satisfy the following requirements:

        • At least three-quarters of the grid should be used.

        • Use different coloured points and lines.

        • Both lines should be smooth curves of best fit through the points.

        • The independent variable is time, and the dependent variable is loss in mass.

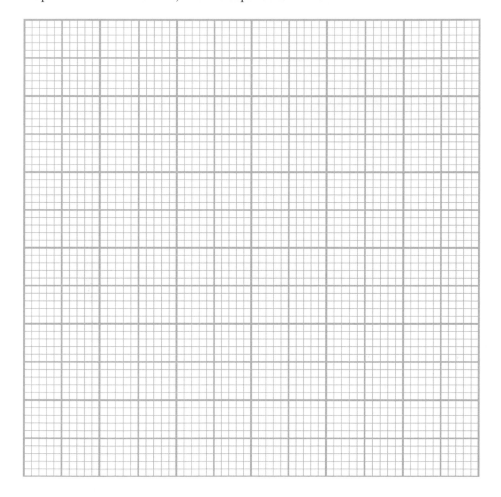

    c   Which pieces gave the faster rate of reaction? Explain how you can tell this from your graph.

        ....

        ....

        ....

7 a What does your answer tell you about the effect of increasing surface area of a solid reactant on the rate of reaction?

....

b Explain why, for both flasks, the same amount of gas is produced at the end of the reaction.

....

> The effect of changing concentration on rate

KEY WORD

concentration: a measure of how much solute is dissolved in a solvent to make a solution. Solutions can be dilute (with a high proportion of the solvent), or concentrated (with a high proportion of the solute)

Exercise 8.2

IN THIS EXERCISE YOU WILL:

- focus on what is meant by solution concentration and how it affects the rate of a reaction

- consider an experiment to find the effect of concentration on rate

- consider a graph to show how the production of a product varies with time

- predict the effects of changing concentration on the shapes of graphs.

Focus

8 Delete the incorrect words to complete the following sentence:

The concentration of a **solution / solvent** is a measure of the number of particles of **solute / solvent** per unit **volume / area**.

9 Figure 8.3 shows three containers. The open circles represent water particles and the closed circles represent hydrochloric acid particles.

Complete the third box by drawing closed circles to represent the hydrochloric acid particles.

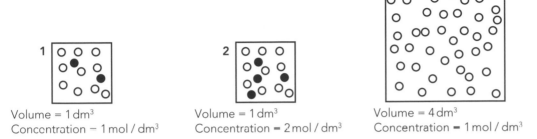

Volume = 1 dm³
Concentration − 1 mol / dm³

Volume = 1 dm³
Concentration = 2 mol / dm³

Volume = 4 dm³
Concentration = 1 mol / dm³

Figure 8.3: Particle diagrams showing water particles (open circles) and hydrochloric acid particles (closed circles).

Practice

10 **a** In the reaction between magnesium and hydrochloric acid solution, the products are magnesium chloride (solution) and hydrogen gas. Write the balanced symbol equation for the reaction.

....

b A group of students were asked to investigate the effect of changing the concentration of acid on the rate of this reaction. The apparatus they used is shown in Figure 8.4.

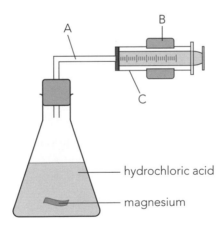

hydrochloric acid

magnesium

Figure 8.4: Collecting hydrogen in a gas syringe.

Give the correct labels for A–C.

A ....   **B** ....   **C** ....

c What measurements would the students make when following the reaction?

....

Challenge

11 The students used 10 cm of magnesium ribbon for their experiments. The graph they obtained for the reaction with 1 mol/dm³ hydrochloric acid is shown in Figure 8.5.

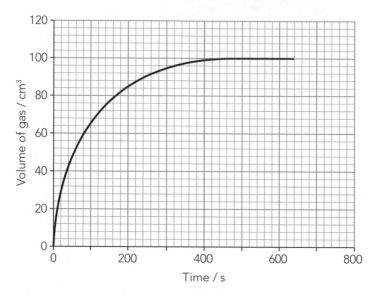

Figure 8.5: Graph to show the volume of hydrogen given off during the reaction of magnesium ribbon with hydrochloric acid.

a   How long does it take to complete the reaction?

....

b   Calculate the mean average rate of gas production for the reaction in cm³/s.

....

....

12 a   Use the axes in Figure 8.5 to draw the graph expected if the concentration of acid was 2 mol/dm³. Label the line you draw as X.

b   Draw the line expected if the concentration of hydrochloric acid was 1 mol/dm³ and the length of magnesium ribbon was reduced to 5 cm.

c   Draw a tangent to the curve X at 100 s and calculate the rate of the reaction at this time.

d   Explain why the reaction slows down as the reaction proceeds.

....

....

....

TIP
Find the slope of the tangent to get the rate.

> Determining how rate of reaction is affected by temperature

KEY WORDS

collision theory: a theory which states that a chemical reaction takes place when particles of the reactants collide with sufficient energy to initiate the reaction

Exercise 8.3

IN THIS EXERCISE YOU WILL:

- describe an experiment designed to investigate the effect of temperature on the rate of a reaction

> explain why temperature affects the rate of a reaction in terms of collision theory.

Focus

13 The reaction between sodium thiosulfate and hydrochloric acid is described in the following word and symbol equations:

sodium thiosulfate (aq) + hydrochloric acid (aq) → water (l) + sulfur dioxide (g) + sulfur (s) + sodium chloride (aq)

.... $Na_2S_2O_3$ + ... $HCl(aq)$ →.... $H_2O(l)$ + ... $SO_2(g)$ + ... $S(s)$ + ... $NaCl(aq)$

a   Balance the symbol equation.

b   Explain why the reaction mixture turns cloudy as the reaction proceeds.

....

....

The method used to follow the course of the reaction is shown in Figure 8.6.

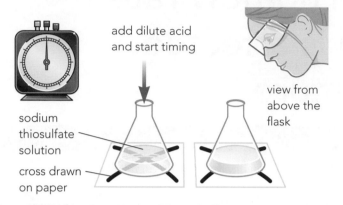

add dilute acid
and start timing

view from
above the
flask

sodium
thiosulfate
solution

cross drawn
on paper

Figure 8.6: The 'disappearing cross' experiment.

c   Describe briefly how the method works.

....

....

d   Comment on what safety precautions are needed and why.

....

....

....

Practice

14 Using the words provided, complete the following paragraph. Note not all of the words are to be used, and one word should be used twice.

> **activation   collide   decreases   frequently   increases   kinetic**
>
> **less   more   potential   quickly   slowly   thermal**

When the temperature of a reaction mixture is increased the particles move around more

.... and this increases their .... energy. Because they move

around more .... at higher temperatures, they collide more ....

and this .... the chance of a reaction taking place. More importantly, when the

particles do .... the collisions are .... efficient. This means that

more collisions have an energy greater than the .... energy, which is the energy

required for reaction to occur.

Challenge

15 Table 8.2 shows the results of experiments as shown in Figure 8.6 carried out at five different temperatures. In each case, 50 cm³ of aqueous sodium thiosulfate was poured into a flask. 10 cm³ of hydrochloric acid was added to the flask. The initial and final temperatures were measured.

    a   Use the thermometer diagrams to record all of the initial and final temperatures in Table 8.2. Complete the table to show the mean average temperatures.

Experiment	Thermometer diagram at start	Initial temperature /°C	Thermometer diagram at end	Final temperature /°C	Mean average temperature /°C	Time for cross to disappear/s
1						130
2						79
3						55
4						33
5						26

Table 8.2: Experimental results.

b Plot a graph of the time taken for the cross to disappear versus the mean average temperature on the grid and draw a smooth line graph.

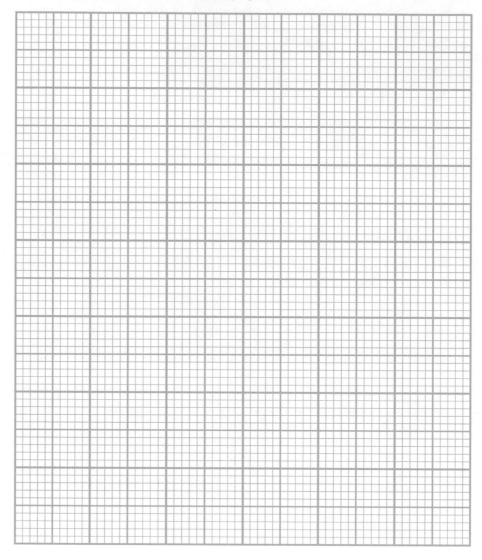

c In which experiment was the speed of reaction greatest? ....

d Explain why the speed was greatest in this experiment.

....

....

....

....

e   Another way of following this reaction is by using a light data-logger. The arrangement used is shown in Figure 8.7. Remember the reaction mixture becomes more cloudy as the reaction proceeds.

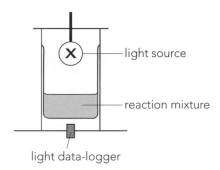

light source

reaction mixture

light data-logger

Figure 8.7: Using a light data-logger for the 'disappearing cross' experiment.

As the reaction proceeds, the reading on the light data-logger changes. Explain why this happens.

....

....

....

....

f   On the axes provided, draw the line you would expect for the reaction.

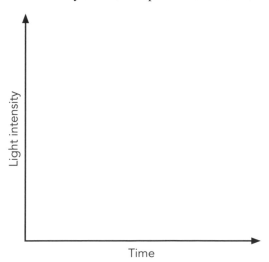

Light intensity

Time

> The effect of catalysts on the reaction rate

KEY WORD
catalyst: a substance that increases the rate of a chemical reaction but itself remains unchanged at the end of the reaction

Exercise 8.4

IN THIS EXERCISE YOU WILL:

- construct a procedure that is designed to show that a catalyst is unchanged in mass
- look at how a catalyst speeds up a chemical reaction

> look at reaction pathway diagrams to further explain the action of catalysts.

Focus

16 Manganese(IV) oxide is an insoluble black solid that catalyses the decomposition of hydrogen peroxide.

Manganese(IV) oxide catalyst

$$2H_2O_2(aq) \xrightarrow{\text{catalyst}} 2H_2O(l) + O_2(g)$$

The following sentences describe a practical investigation designed to show that after catalysing the reaction, the manganese(IV) oxide is unchanged in mass. The sentences are not in the correct order. Using the letters next to each sentence, put the actions in the correct order.

P	Once the reaction is finished, the mixture is filtered through the weighed filter paper.
Q	The manganese(IV) oxide is added to some hydrogen peroxide in a boiling tube and the oxygen given off is tested for using a glowing spill.
R	The dried manganese(IV) oxide and filter paper is weighed.
S	The weight of the dried manganese(IV) oxide and filter paper is compared with their combined mass at the beginning.
T	The manganese(IV) oxide and filter paper are placed in an oven and left to dry.
U	Some manganese(IV) oxide is weighed out and the mass noted.
V	All the manganese(IV) oxide is washed from the boiling tube and filtered through the weighed filter paper.
W	A filter paper is weighed and its mass noted.

Correct order:

....

> **TIP**
>
> When you put an investigation in order, you must check your answer. Imagine yourself going through each step.

Practice

17 In this exercise you will look at a reaction that is sped up by different substances. Catalysts will speed up chemical reactions and are *unchanged chemically* at the end of the reaction. False catalysts also speed up the reaction but are *changed chemically* at the end of the reaction.

Zinc reacts with sulfuric acid to form hydrogen gas and zinc sulfate solution. The substances investigated as catalysts were copper metal (pink–brown solid) and blue copper(II) sulfate solution. The speed of the reaction was monitored by observing the bubbles of hydrogen gas formed. The results are shown in Table 8.3.

Tube	Contents	Observations
A	zinc granule + sulfuric acid	a few bubbles
B	zinc granule + sulfuric acid + copper metal	rapid evolution of bubbles, and the copper metal unchanged in appearance and mass after drying
C	zinc granule + sulfuric acid + few drops of copper(II) sulfate solution	rapid evolution of bubbles, and a pink–brown solid formed

Table 8.3: Observations when zinc reacts with sulfuric acid.

a Which of the two substances, copper or copper(II) sulfate, is not a catalyst for the reaction even though it speeds up the reaction (false catalyst)?

Answer ....

Explanation

....

....

....

b Which of the two substances, copper or copper(II) sulfate, is a true catalyst for the reaction?

Answer ....

Explanation

....

....

....

Challenge

18 A catalyst speeds up a reaction by reducing the activation energy of the reaction.

a On the diagram in Figure 8.8:

- draw the reaction pathway for the uncatalysed reaction between the zinc and sulfuric acid

- label the activation energy for this uncatalysed reaction

- label the enthalpy change for the reaction.

b On the same diagram:

- draw the reaction pathway for the catalysed reaction

- label the activation energy for the catalysed reaction.

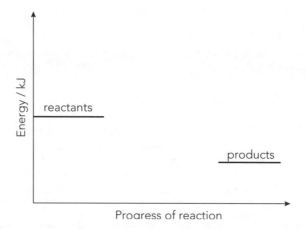

Figure 8.8: Reaction pathway diagram for a catalysed reaction.

PEER ASSESSMENT

With your partner, look at all the exercises in this chapter and consider the following:

1 If there is one exercise that you understood and got correct but your partner did not, explain to them how you understood it. Then reverse the roles so that they can explain one to you.

2 Look at exercise(s) that you both did not understand. What do you need to do in order to improve your understanding?

> Chapter 9

Reversible reactions and equilibrium

› Exploiting reversible reactions

KEY WORDS

dehydration: a chemical reaction in which water is removed from a compound

hydrated salts: salts whose crystals contain combined water (*water of crystallisation*) as part of the structure

reversible reaction: a chemical reaction that can go either forwards or backwards, depending on the conditions

Exercise 9.1

IN THIS EXERCISE YOU WILL:

- review the properties of reversible reactions

- describe how some reactions can be reversed by a change in conditions, particularly those involving the dehydration of hydrated salts

- investigate how some reversible reactions can be used as tests for the presence of water.

Focus

1   Hydrated cobalt(II) chloride is a pink crystalline salt. When heated it is dehydrated to a form which is blue.

$$CoCl_2 \cdot 6H_2O \xrightarrow{\text{heat}} CoCl_2 + 6H_2O$$

pink   blue

a   Is this reaction exothermic or endothermic? ....

b   How could you change the blue form of the salt back to pink cobalt(II) chloride?

....

....

c   Explain how you can tell that the reaction from blue cobalt(II) chloride to pink cobalt(II) chloride is exothermic.

....

....

d   What adjective, meaning 'without water', can be used to describe the blue form of this salt?

....

Practice

2   Crystals of copper(II) sulfate can be dehydrated by heating in a similar way to cobalt(II) chloride. This dehydration can also be reversed.

a   Complete the following equation that summarises these two reactions, and enter the colours of the two forms beneath the equation:

$$CuSO_4 \cdot 5H_2O \quad \rightleftharpoons \quad \text{................} + \text{.....} H_2O$$

....

b   What is the meaning of the symbol $\rightleftharpoons$ in this equation?

....

c   What observations would you see if some drops of a liquid made up of 10% ethanol and 90% water were added to the dehydrated form of copper(II) sulfate ($CuSO_4$)? Explain your reasoning.

....

....

....

....

d   How would you test to see if a sample of liquid is pure water?

....

> TIP
>
> These chemical tests are for the presence of water in a liquid sample; they do not prove that the water is pure.

Challenge

3   The enthalpy change for the dehydration of copper(II) sulfate is $+75.3\,\text{kJ/mol}$.

a   What is the enthalpy change for the backwards reaction? ....

b   If water is added back to $CuSO_4(s)$, does the temperature increase or decrease?

     ....

c   Explain your answer.

     ....

     ....

d   On the reaction pathway diagram in Figure 9.1, insert the following labels and arrows:

   • $CuSO_4(s) + 5H_2O(l)$

   • $CuSO_4 \cdot 5H_2O$

   • activation energy

   • enthalpy change of reaction.

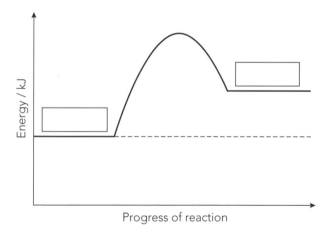

Figure 9.1: Reaction pathway diagram.

4 The following statements concern the properties of reversible reactions. Tick the appropriate boxes to state whether the statements are true or false.

	True	False
All reactions are easily reversible.		
Reversible reactions are represented by the arrows $\rightleftharpoons$.		
When the concentrations of reactants and products are equal, reversible reactions stop.		
If the forward reaction is endothermic, the backward reaction is exothermic.		
Heating always favours the endothermic reaction in a reversible reaction.		
When equilibrium is reached, reversible reactions stop.		
Reversible reactions can go forwards or backwards depending on the conditions.		

Table 9.1: The properties of reversible reactions.

> Fertilisers

KEY WORDS

compound fertiliser: a fertiliser such as a NPK fertiliser or nitrochalk that contains more than one compound to provide elements to the soil

fertiliser: a substance added to the soil to replace essential elements lost when crops are harvested, which enables crops to grow faster and increases the yield

Exercise 9.2

IN THIS EXERCISE YOU WILL:

- understand how certain elements are particularly important for plant growth

- learn how fertilisers are produced to add nutrients back to soil to promote crop growth

- review relative molecular masses and relative atomic masses.

Focus

5   The most important use of ammonia is in fertiliser production. Fertilisers are added to the soil to improve crop yields.

Using the words provided, complete the following paragraph about fertilisers.

ammonium   elements   fertilisers   nutrients   phosphate

phosphorus   proteins   salts

Crop plants are found to need three elements for healthy growth: nitrogen (N),

.... (P) and potassium (K). Plants take up these elements in the form of

.... such as ....nitrate, potassium nitrate, and potassium or

ammonium .... These ....are needed for the new plants to make

the .... needed for growth. Farmers add ....to the soil to replace

the .... that previous crops have absorbed during growth.

Practice

6   A flowchart for making different fertilisers industrially is shown in Figure 9.2.

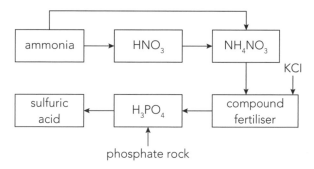

Figure 9.2: Flowchart for the industrial production of ammonium nitrate and a compound fertiliser.

a   What is the chemical formula for ammonia? ....

b   Give the names of the following compounds shown in Figure 9.2.

KCl .... HNO_3 ....

H_3PO_4 .... NH_4NO_3 ....

c   Name the acid and alkali that could be used to make the following fertilisers.

potassium phosphate:

....

ammonium sulfate:

....

d   Give the word and balanced symbol equations for the reaction between ammonia and nitric acid.

word equation:

....

balanced symbol equation (including state symbols):

....

Challenge

7   Ammonium chloride is a fertiliser used for alkaline soils. The decomposition of ammonium chloride to form ammonia and hydrogen chloride is reversible.

The equation for the reaction is:

$NH_4Cl(s) \rightleftharpoons NH_3(g) + HCl(g)$

A teacher discussed the reversible reaction with her students. The apparatus she used to show the forward reaction is shown in Figure 9.3.

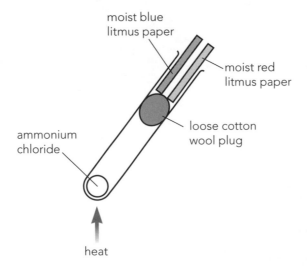

Figure 9.3: Heating ammonium chloride.

After heating the ammonium chloride, the blue litmus paper turned red and the red litmus paper turned blue showing that ammonia and hydrogen chloride are formed. This experiment shows that the forward reaction is endothermic.

a   In which direction does the $NH_3(g) + HCl(g) \rightleftharpoons NH_4Cl(s)$ reversible reaction move when cooled: forwards or backwards?

....

A mixture of ammonia, hydrogen chloride and ammonium chloride can be set up at equilibrium in a closed syringe (Figure 9.4).

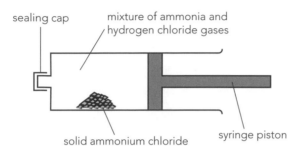

sealing cap   mixture of ammonia and hydrogen chloride gases

solid ammonium chloride   syringe piston

Figure 9.4: A mixture at equilibrium in a closed syringe.

b **i**   What can you say about the forward and reverse reactions at equilibrium?

....

....

ii   What would happen to the equilibrium if the pressure in the syringe were decreased?

....

....

iii Explain your answer to part **ii**.

....

....

....

> Reversible reactions in industry

KEY WORDS

closed system: a system where none of the reactants or products can escape the reaction mixture or the container where the reaction is taking place

dynamic (chemical) equilibrium: two chemical reactions, one the reverse of the other, taking place at the same time, where the concentrations of the reactants and products remain constant because the rate at which the forward reaction occurs is the same as that of the reverse reaction

Exercise 9.3

IN THIS EXERCISE YOU WILL:

> review the effects of changing conditions on the position of equilibrium in a reversible reaction

> investigate how ammonia is produced industrially in the Haber process

> evaluate data concerning the conditions used in the making of ammonia

> review the conditions used in the Contact process for the production of sulfuric acid.

> Focus

8   Table 9.2 summarises the effects of various changes in conditions on any reversible reaction at equilibrium in a closed system. Complete Table 9.2 by deleting the incorrect words in the right-hand column for each change in conditions.

Change in conditions	Effect on the position of the equilibrium
Increase in pressure for reactions involving gases	Equilibrium shifts to favour the side of the reaction with **more / fewer** gas molecules (the side which occupies **more / less** space).
Decrease in pressure for reactions involving gases	Equilibrium shifts to favour the side of the reaction with **more / fewer** gas molecules (the side which occupies **more / less** space).
Increase in temperature for any reaction	Equilibrium shifts to favour the **exothermic / endothermic** reaction.
Decrease in temperature for any reaction	Equilibrium shifts to favour the **exothermic / endothermic** reaction.
Addition of a catalyst	Forward and reverse reactions both sped up so no effect on equilibrium position, but the reaction reaches equilibrium **slower / faster**.

Table 9.2: The effect of changing conditions on the equilibrium position of a reaction.

Practice

9   The Contact process for the production of sulfuric acid is another important industrial process based on a reversible reaction. In the converter, sulfur dioxide and oxygen are passed over a series of catalyst beds at a temperature of about 450 °C.

$$2SO_2(g) + O_2(g) \rightleftharpoons 2SO_3(g) \quad \Delta H = -197\,kJ$$

a   What is the catalyst used in the Contact process? ....

b   An increase in pressure increases the yield of sulfur trioxide. Explain the reason for this effect.

....

....

....

c   Even though an increase in pressure increases the yield of sulfur trioxide, the reaction in the converter is carried out at about 2 atmospheres pressure. Suggest reasons why high pressures are avoided in industry unless absolutely necessary.

....

....

Challenge

10 The industrial production of ammonia is highly important and an illustration of the effect of changing physical conditions on the equilibrium position of a reversible reaction in a closed system.

> **TIP**
>
> At chemical equilibrium the forward and reverse reactions are taking place at the same time, and their rates are equal. The concentrations of the reactants and products are no longer changing.

Ammonia is made by the Haber process using an iron catalyst.

$N_2 + 3H_2 \rightleftharpoons 2NH_3$ (The forward reaction is exothermic.)

a   State the conditions of temperature and pressure used for the Haber process.

....

b Sketch a reaction pathway diagram to show both the catalysed and the uncatalysed reaction. Label the diagram to show the following key features: the reactants and products, the enthalpy change for the reaction, and the catalysed and uncatalysed reactions.

PEER ASSESSMENT

Compare your answer to question **10b** with a partner. Discuss the labelling of the different features of the diagram, looking in particular at the effect of adding a catalyst and how this change is brought about. Is there anything you need to change on your diagram following your discussion? Do you find this type of discussion with a partner helpful?

---

11 Table 9.3 shows how the percentage of ammonia in the mixture leaving the reaction vessel varies under different conditions.

Pressure / kPa	10 000	20 000	30 000	40 000
% of ammonia at 300 °C	45	65	72	78
% of ammonia at 500 °C	9	18	25	31

Table 9.3: Data on the yield of ammonia with changing conditions.

a Use the grid to plot graphs of the percentage of ammonia against pressure at both 300 °C and 500 °C.

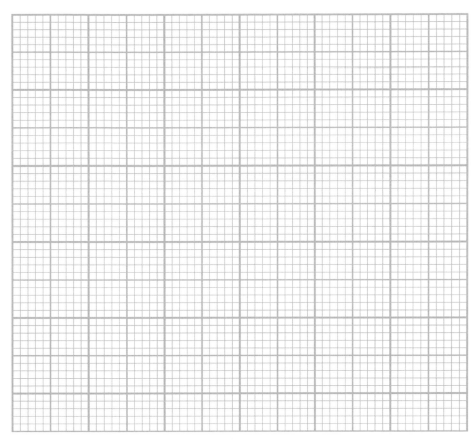

b What is the percentage of ammonia formed at 25 000 kPa and 300 °C?

....

c Use your graphs to estimate the percentage of ammonia formed at 400 °C and 25 000 kPa.

....

d The advantage of using a low temperature is the large percentage of ammonia formed. What is the disadvantage of using a low temperature?

....

....

....

e Suggest two advantages of using high pressure in the manufacture of ammonia.

....

....

....

> Chapter 10

Redox reactions

> Understanding oxidation and reduction

> **KEY WORDS**
>
> **oxidation:** there are three definitions of oxidation:
> i   a reaction in which oxygen is added to an element or compound
> ii   a reaction involving the loss of electrons from an atom, molecule or ion
> iii   a reaction in which the oxidation state of an element is increased
>
> **redox reaction:** a reaction involving both reduction and oxidation
>
> **reduction:** there are three definitions of reduction:
> i   a reaction in which oxygen is removed from a compound
> ii   a reaction involving the gain of electrons by an atom, molecule or ion
> iii   a reaction in which the oxidation state of an element is decreased

Exercise 10.1

> **IN THIS EXERCISE YOU WILL:**
>
> • define oxidation and reduction in terms of the addition or removal of oxygen
>
> • identify the compound that has been oxidised or reduced in a given chemical reaction
>
> • practise balancing symbol equations
>
> > describe oxidising and reducing agents in the context of redox reactions.

Focus

1 a Complete Figure 10.1 to show what substances are used and what is produced in burning and rusting.

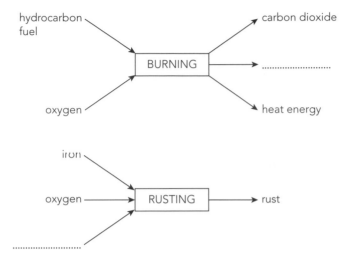

Figure 10.1: Reactions involving oxygen.

b What type of chemical change is involved in both of the reactions shown in Figure 10.1?

....

2 Oxidation and reduction reactions are important. There are several definitions of oxidation and reduction. Complete the following statements.

a If a substance gains oxygen during a reaction, it is ....

b If a substance .... oxygen during a reaction, it is reduced.

c The substance that gives oxygen to another substance in a chemical reaction is the

.... agent.

d The substance that accepts oxygen from another substance in a chemical reaction is the

.... agent.

Practice

3   Figure 10.2 shows (a) the oxidation of copper to copper(II) oxide and (b) the reduction of copper oxide back to copper using hydrogen.

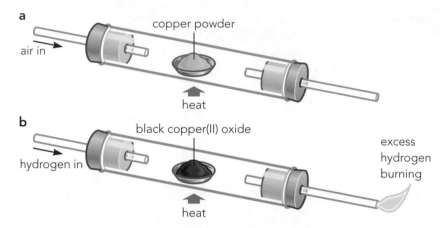

Figure 10.2: Oxidation and reduction reactions involving copper.

a   Fill in the boxes in Figure 10.3 with the appropriate terms.

$$\text{copper(II) oxide} + \text{hydrogen} \xrightarrow{\text{heat}} \text{copper} + \text{water}$$

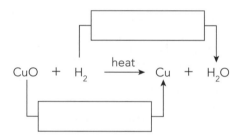

Figure 10.3: An oxidation and reduction reaction.

b   What type of agent is hydrogen acting as in this reaction?

....

c   Equations **i–iv** show unbalanced symbol equations that represent redox reactions involving metal oxides and other substances. For each reaction:

   •   if necessary, balance the equation

   •   put a ring around the oxidising agent

   •   underline the reducing agent.

   i   ....$Zn(s)$ + ...$Ag_2O(s)$ → ....$ZnO(s)$ + ...$Ag(s)$
   ii   ....$Fe_2O_3(s)$ + ...$Al(s)$ → ....$Fe(s)$ + ...$Al_2O_3(s)$
   iii   ....$Mg(s)$ + ...$Al_2O_3(s)$ → ....$MgO(s)$ + ...$Al(s)$
   iv   ....$CO_2(g)$ + ...$Mg(s)$ → ....$C(s)$ + ...$MgO(s)$

Challenge

4   Catalytic converters (Figure 10.4) reduce the pollution from motor vehicles by converting polluting gases in the exhaust fumes into less harmful gases.

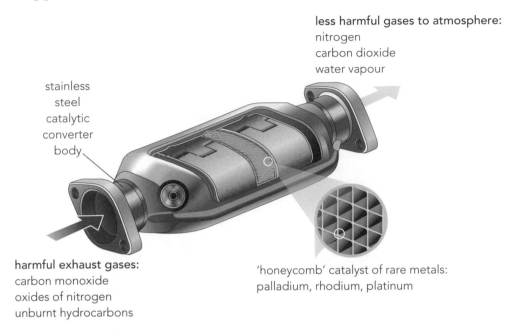

less harmful gases to atmosphere:
nitrogen
carbon dioxide
water vapour

stainless
steel
catalytic
converter
body

harmful exhaust gases:
carbon monoxide
oxides of nitrogen
unburnt hydrocarbons

'honeycomb' catalyst of rare metals:
palladium, rhodium, platinum

Figure 10.4: A catalytic converter.

Car exhaust fumes contain gases such as carbon monoxide (CO), nitrogen monoxide (nitrogen(II) oxide, NO) and unburnt hydrocarbons. The catalytic converter converts these to carbon dioxide CO_2), nitrogen (N_2) and water (H_2O) in reactions such as those shown here (a–c):

For each reaction, explain why it is a redox reaction and identify the oxidising and reducing agents.

a   carbon monoxide + oxygen → carbon dioxide

$$2CO(g) + O_2(g) \rightarrow 2CO_2(g)$$

....

....

b   nitrogen monoxide + carbon monoxide → nitrogen + carbon dioxide

$$2NO(g) + 2CO(g) \rightarrow N_2(g) + 2CO_2(g)$$

....

....

c   hydrocarbons + oxygen → carbon dioxide + water

One of the unburnt hydrocarbons from the fuel could be heptane. Complete the balanced symbol equation for the reaction for heptane.

C_7H_{16} + ... O_2 → 7 .... + $8H_2O$

....

....

> TIP
>
> In a chemical reaction both oxidation and reduction must take place at the same time. This is why the term redox reaction is used. In such a reaction the oxidising agent brings about oxidation but is itself reduced in the process.

> Extending the definitions of oxidation and reduction

> KEY WORDS
>
> **half-equations:** ionic equations showing the reactions at the anode (oxidation) and cathode (reduction) in an electrolytic cell
>
> **halogen displacement reactions:** reactions in which a more reactive halogen displaces a less reactive halogen from a solution of its salt

Exercise 10.2

> IN THIS EXERCISE YOU WILL:
>
> > extend the definitions of oxidation and reduction to reactions is which there is loss and gain of electrons by the reactants
>
> > relate the transfer of electrons from one element to another as a redox reaction
>
> > practise the use and balancing of half-equations, including electrode reactions in electrolysis and relate these to reduction and oxidation
>
> > consider displacement reactions as redox reactions
>
> > apply the extended definitions to a test for reducing agents and halogen displacement reactions.

Focus

5 a A further definition of redox reactions links oxidation and reduction to the exchange of electrons during a reaction.

Complete the following statements.

i Oxidation is the .... of electrons.

ii Reduction is the .... of electrons.

> **TIP**
>
> Use the mnemonic 'OIL RIG' to help remember the difference between oxidation and reduction in terms of electron transfer.

b The following two electronic configurations shown illustrate the changes taking place when metals and non-metals react to form ions.

For each reaction:

- fill in the gap in the space above the arrow
- explain why it is a redox reaction
- identify the oxidising and reducing agents.

Transfer .... e^-

i Sodium (Na) 2,8,1 ⟶ Chlorine (Cl) 2,8,7

Sodium ion (Na^+) 2,8   Chloride ion (Cl^-) 2,8,8

Explanation: ....

....

Transfer .... e^-

ii Calcium (Ca) 2,8,8,2 ⟶ Oxygen (O) 2,6

Calcium ion (Ca^{2+}) 2,8   Oxide ion (O^{2-}) 2,8

Explanation: ....

....

Practice

6 a Fill in the boxes on the ionic equation (Figure 10.5) with the appropriate terms.

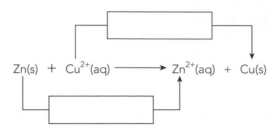

$$Zn(s) + Cu^{2+}(aq) \longrightarrow Zn^{2+}(aq) + Cu(s)$$

Figure 10.5: Ionic equation for the reaction between zinc and copper(II) ions.

What type of agent are copper(II) ions acting as in this reaction? ....

b Balance the following two ionic equations. Under each reactant write either reducing agent (RA) or oxidising agent (OA).

i .....$Cu(s) + 2Ag^+(aq) \rightarrow$.....$Cu^{2+}(aq) + 2Ag(s)$

....

ii .....$Mg(s) +$.....$Al^{3+}(aq) \rightarrow$.....$Mg^{2+}(aq) +$.....$Al(s)$

....

c Electrode reactions take place at the anode and the cathode during electrolysis. The half-equations **i–iii** show reactions that take place at the anode and cathode. For each reaction:

*   balance the equation
*   give the electrode at which the reaction takes place
*   state whether it is reduction or oxidation that takes place.

i $Cu^{2+}(aq) +$.................$e^- \rightarrow Cu(s)$

Electrode = ...   Type of reaction = ...

ii .....$Cl^-(aq) \rightarrow Cl_2(g) +$.................$e^-$

Electrode = ...   Type of reaction = ...

iii $Al^{3+}(l) +$.................$e^- \rightarrow Al(l)$

Electrode = ...   Type of reaction = ...

TIP

The redox reactions taking place in electrolytic cells are the only time when the processes of oxidation and reduction in an overall reaction are separated: reduction always takes place at the cathode, and oxidation always takes place at the anode.

PEER ASSESSMENT

Go through Exercise 10.2 with a partner. Did both of you understand the new definitions of oxidation and reduction? Can you come up with an easy memory aid?

For example, *if an atom or ion loses electrons it becomes more … and if it gains electrons it becomes more …*

Check your answers to see if you have understood the new way of looking at redox reactions. If you applied your memory aid, did it work?

Challenge

7   Potassium iodide is a reducing agent and can be used to identify redox reactions. Potassium iodide solution is colourless but when reduced some yellow–brown iodine is formed.

$$2I^-(aq) \quad \rightarrow \quad I_2(aq) + 2e^-$$

colourless   yellow

One such reaction is that between potassium iodide solution and chlorine water.

chlorine + potassium iodide → iodine + potassium chloride

   a   Write the balanced symbol equation for this reaction (including state symbols).

....

   b   Give the ionic equation for the reaction between chlorine and iodide ions.

....

   c   What has been reduced in this reaction?

....

   d   Give the half-equation for this reduction.

....

8   This type of reaction can be called a halogen displacement reaction. The halogens – chlorine, bromine and iodine – differ in terms of their ability to displace another halogen from a solution of its salt.

Write the ionic equation for the reaction of chlorine with potassium bromide.

....

> Oxidation numbers

KEY WORDS

oxidation: there are three definitions of oxidation:
i   a reaction in which oxygen is added to an element or compound
ii a reaction involving the loss of electrons from an atom, molecule or ion
iii a reaction in which the oxidation state of an element is increased

reduction: there are three definitions of reduction:
i   a reaction in which oxygen is removed from a compound
ii a reaction involving the gain of electrons by an atom, molecule or ion
iii a reaction in which the oxidation state of an element is decreased

Exercise 10.3

IN THIS EXERCISE YOU WILL:

- describe how a Roman numeral is used to show the oxidation number of an element in a compound

  > develop the broadest definition of redox in terms of an increase or decrease in the oxidation number of atoms present in the reactants

  > learn how to give the oxidation number of a given atom in an element or compound

  > apply an understanding of oxidation and reduction to electrode reactions in a hydrogen–oxygen fuel cell.

TIP

Have in mind the following values shown.

Element	Oxidation number in compound
Oxygen	–2 except in peroxides
Hydrogen	+1 unless it is in a metal hydride
Fluorine	always –1
Metals in binary compounds	+ whatever the charge is on the ion

Focus

9   The oxidation number of an element gives us an indication of how oxidised or reduced a particular element is in a compound. What is the oxidation number of the metal in the following compounds?

a   copper(II) chloride ....

b   iron(III) oxide ....

c   iron(II) sulfate ....

d   manganese(IV) oxide ....

10   The oxidation number can just be the charge on the ion in an ionic compound; in copper(II) sulfate the copper ion is Cu^{2+}. However, we can use oxidation numbers in more complex situations. In potassium manganate(VII), for instance, the oxidation number of manganese is +7.

What is the oxidation number of the underlined element in the following elements or compounds?

a $\underline{Fe}Cl_3$ ....

b $\underline{N}_2$ ....

c $\underline{Al}Cl_3$ ....

d $K_2\underline{Cr}_2O_7$ ....

e $H_2\underline{S}O_4$ ....

f $\underline{Cu}_2O$ ....

Practice

11   Burning magnesium will react with carbon dioxide to produce carbon.

a   Write the oxidation numbers of each element, except oxygen, beneath each formula in the following equation.

$$2Mg(s) + CO_2(g) \rightarrow 2MgO(s) + C(s)$$

    ....

b   Use oxidation numbers to state which elements have been oxidised and which have been reduced in this reaction (give the values for each change).

....

....

12 Acidified potassium manganate(VII) solution is an oxidising agent and can be used as a test to identify redox reactions. If this solution is added to an unknown liquid and a reducing agent is present then the manganate(VII) is decolourised. Complete the following summary of the change for the manganate(VII) ions.

$$MnO_4^- \qquad \rightarrow \qquad Mn^{2+}$$

oxidation number: ....

colour: ....

Challenge

13 Oxidation and reduction reactions also take place in electrochemical and electrolytic cells. Electrons are either gained or lost at the electrodes.

The hydrogen–oxygen fuel cell is an increasingly important way to generate electrical energy to power vehicles rather than gasoline (petrol). The structure of a typical fuel cell using an alkaline electrolyte is shown in Figure 10.6.

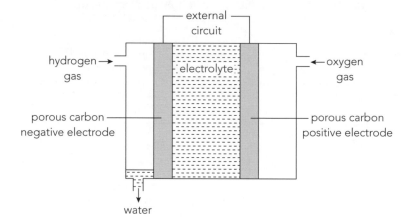

Figure 10.6: An alkaline hydrogen–oxygen fuel cell.

a The reaction taking place in such a fuel cell is the combustion of hydrogen. Write the overall equation for that reaction.

....

b   The equation for the reaction at the negative electrode is:

$H_2(g) + 2OH^-(aq) \rightarrow 2H_2O(l) + 2e^-$

What type of reaction is this? Explain your answer.

....

c   At the positive electrode oxygen molecules react with water molecules and gain electrons to form hydroxide ions. Complete the following ionic equation for this reaction.

$O_2(g) + ...H_2O(l) + ...e^- \rightarrow 4OH^-(aq)$

d   By combining the two half-equations taking place at the electrodes, show that the overall equation for the fuel cell is that of the reaction you gave in **a**. Show your working.

....

....

....

....

e   Describe two advantages of using hydrogen as a fuel rather than gasoline (petrol).

....

....

f   Suggest one disadvantage of using hydrogen as a fuel.

....

Chapter 11

Acids and bases

> The pH values of acids and bases and their effects on indicators

KEY WORDS

acid: a substance that dissolves in water, producing $H^+(aq)$ ions – a solution of an acid turns litmus red and has a pH below 7.
Acids act as proton donors

alkali: a soluble base that produces $OH^-(aq)$ ions in water – a solution of an alkali turns litmus blue and has a pH above 7

base: a substance that neutralises an acid, producing a salt and water as the only products. Bases act as proton acceptors

indicator: a substance which changes colour when added to acidic or alkaline solutions, e.g. litmus or thymolphthalein

litmus: the most common indicator; turns red in acid and blue in alkali

methyl orange: an acid–base indicator that is red in acidic and yellow in alkaline solutions

pH scale: a scale running from below 0 to 14, used for expressing the acidity or alkalinity of a solution; a neutral solution has a pH of 7

thymolphthalein: an acid–base indicator that is colourless in acidic solutions and blue in alkaline solutions

universal indicator: a mixture of indicators that has different colours in solutions of different pH

Exercise 11.1

IN THIS EXERCISE YOU WILL:

- focus on the differences between acids and alkalis in terms of the pH values of their solutions

- learn the formulae of some common laboratory acids and alkalis

- consider how the pH of the solution will tell you how acidic or how alkaline a solution is

- describe the colours of different indicators under acid, neutral and alkaline conditions

- relate the colours of universal indicator to the pH value of a solution.

Focus

1   Using the words provided, complete the following paragraph. Note that not all the words should be used, and one word should be used twice.

> acids   alkalis   greater   hydrochloric   hydrogen   hydroxide   insoluble
>
> less   nitric   oxides   potassium   sodium   soluble   sulfuric   water

Acids are substances that dissolve in .... to give a solution with a pH

.... than 7. .... acid has the formula HCl and is a strong acid.

.... acid (formula = H_2SO_4) and .... acid (formula = HNO_3) are

also strong .... In acidic solutions the concentration of the ....

ions is greater than the concentration of .... ions.

Bases are the .... and hydroxides of metals and ammonia. A base will neutralise

an acid to form a salt and ....

Most bases are .... in water, but alkalis are bases that are .... in

water and their solutions have pH values .... than 7. KOH (.........................

hydroxide) and NaOH (......................... hydroxide) are both strong .... In

alkaline solutions the concentration of .... ions is greater than the concentration

of .... ions.

Practice

2   Look at the statements in Table 11.1. Each statement describes either an acid, a base or an alkali. Put
a tick in the correct column for each statement. One row of the table has been completed as an example.

Practical observation	Acid	Base	Alkali
A solution of the substance has a pH of 8.			
A solution of the substance turns litmus paper blue.			✓
A solution of the substance turns litmus paper red.			
A substance that neutralises an acid but is insoluble in water.			
A substance that neutralises an acid and is soluble in water.			
A substance that is an insoluble oxide or hydroxide of a metal.			
A substance that is a soluble hydroxide of a metal.			
A solution with a pH of 9 that is produced when ammonia is dissolved in water.			
A solution of the substance has a pH of 3.			
A solution of the substance has a pH of 13.			

Table 11.1: Statements about acids, bases and alkalis.

Challenge

3   The graph in Figure 11.1 shows what happens to the pH values if sodium hydroxide solution (an
alkali) is added to a solution of hydrochloric acid. Samples of the mixture are removed on a glass
rod at points A, B and C and spotted onto universal indicator paper.

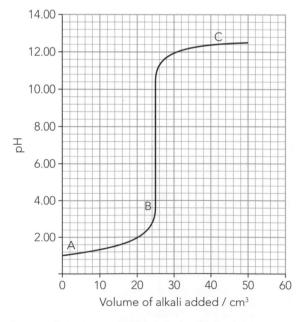

Figure 11.1: pH when different volumes of alkali are added to hydrochloric acid.

a   What is the colour of the universal indicator at A, B and C?

Colour at A:

....

Colour at B:

....

Colour at C:

....

b   What would be the colours of thymolphthalein and methyl orange at pH 12?

Colour of thymolphthalein:

....

Colour of methyl orange:

....

c   On the graph, mark with an N where the acid is neutralised by the alkali.

d   What is the volume of alkali needed to neutralise the acid?

....

e   What is the best apparatus to add the alkali accurately to the acid?

....

f   What is the pH of the solution when $15\,cm^3$ of alkali have been added?

....

> The reactions of acids

KEY WORDS
antacids: compounds used medically to treat indigestion by neutralising excess stomach acid
salts: ionic compounds made by the neutralisation of an acid with a base (or alkali), e.g. copper(II) sulfate and potassium nitrate

Exercise 11.2

IN THIS EXERCISE YOU WILL:

- reinforce your knowledge of acids

- consider the reactions of acids with reactive metals, metal oxides, metal hydroxides and metal carbonates

- write the word and balanced symbol equations for these reactions

- predict the products of the reactions of acids

- interpret observations of the reactions of acids.

Focus

4 The boxes on the left-hand side describe the reactions of acids with different substances. On the right-hand side are statements about these reactions. Draw lines from the left-hand side to the statements that are true about these reactions. Note that more than one line can be drawn from each type of reaction.

Type of reaction	Statements about these reactions
Acid + metal carbonate	Gives H_2 gas as a product
	Gives a salt + water + a gas as the products
Acid + reactive metal	Gives CO_2 as a product
	Does give an effervescence (fizzing)
Acid + insoluble metal oxide	Gives a salt and water as the only products
Acid + alkali	Gives a salt and gas only

Practice

5   Table 11.2 gives the formulae of some different acids, bases, reactive metals, reactive metal carbonates and salts. Use this information to write the word and balanced symbol equations for the reactions **a–f**.

Acid	Base/reactive metal	Carbonate	Salt
HNO_3	NaOH	$CaCO_3$	$CaCl_2$
HCl	$Ca(OH)_2$	Na_2CO_3	NaCl
H_2SO_4	CaO		$NaNO_3$
	Mg		Na_2SO_4
			$Ca(NO_3)_2$
			$MgCl_2$

Table 11.2: Formulae of different acids, bases, reactive metal carbonates and salts.

a   magnesium + hydrochloric acid

Word equation:

....

Symbol equation:

....

b   calcium hydroxide + hydrochloric acid

Word equation:

....

Symbol equation:

....

c   calcium oxide + nitric acid

Word equation:

....

Symbol equation:

....

d   sodium hydroxide + sulfuric acid

Word equation:

....

Symbol equation:

....

e   sodium carbonate + nitric acid

Word equation:

....

Symbol equation:

....

f   magnesium + nitric acid

Word equation:

....

Symbol equation:

....

Challenge

6   Antacids are widely used in medicine to overcome the discomfort and problems caused by too much acid in our stomachs.

A group of students were given the task of investigating the effectiveness of two substances as antacids. The two substances to be investigated were magnesium hydroxide and magnesium carbonate.

The students were given the following apparatus and chemicals:

- two spatulas
- exactly 2 g of each substance in powder form
- 250 cm^3 of 0.1 mol/dm^3 hydrochloric acid
- a 50 cm^3 burette, conical flasks, a white tile
- access to distilled water
- methyl orange indicator.

Give the balanced symbol equations for the two reactions taking place.

a   For magnesium hydroxide:

....

b   For magnesium carbonate:

....

c Describe how the students could carry out their investigation using the apparatus and chemicals listed.

....

....

....

....

....

....

....

....

....

....

d If the magnesium carbonate were used as an antacid, the user might experience some additional discomfort. Explain why.

....

....

TIP

The number of marks available for a question can help you understand the number of points you need to make in your answer.

> Acid–alkali titrations

KEY WORDS

burette: a piece of glass apparatus used for delivering a variable volume of liquid accurately

volumetric pipette: a pipette used to measure out a volume of solution accurately

Exercise 11.3

IN THIS EXERCISE YOU WILL:

- revise neutralisation

- revise the apparatus you use to carry out titrations

- practise reading the apparatus

- consider why an indicator is required for the experiments

- use a titration method to compare the concentrations of two different hydrochloric acid solutions

- interpret experimental data to predict a neutralising volume.

Focus

7 A student investigated an aqueous solution of sodium hydroxide and its reaction with hydrochloric acid using a titration method. The procedure used is described in the following paragraphs. Delete the incorrect words to complete the paragraphs.

a Experiment 1

Using a **beaker / volumetric pipette**, $10\,cm^3$ of the sodium hydroxide solution was placed in a **conical / round-bottomed** flask. Thymolphthalein indicator was added to the flask turning the solution **red / blue** because of the **acidic / alkaline** conditions. A **burette / volumetric pipette** was filled to the **0.0 / 50.0** cm^3 mark with hydrochloric acid (solution P). The acid was then run into the flask until the colour changed to **red / colourless** showing that the alkali in the flask had been **neutralised / naturalised** by the acid.

The volume of **acid / alkali** added was noted. The flask was washed thoroughly with **tap / distilled** water.

b Experiment 2

The experiment was repeated using the same volume of sodium hydroxide **acid / alkali** in the flask but a different solution of acid (solution Q) in the **burette / volumetric pipette**.

c During both titrations, the flask was placed on a white tile. Explain why this white tile was used.

....

....

....

Practice

8 **a** Use the burette diagram (Figure 11.2) and record the volume in the results table (Table 11.3) for experiment 1 (acid solution P).

   b Figure 11.3 shows the results from the titration for experiment 2 (acid solution Q). Use this diagram to complete Table 11.3.

Figure 11.2: Burette diagram – experiment 1.

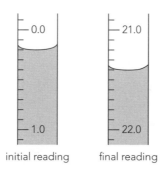

initial reading   final reading

Figure 11.3: Burette diagram – experiment 2.

Burette readings	Experiment 1 / cm³	Experiment 2 / cm³
Final reading		
Initial reading	0.0	
Difference		

Table 11.3: Burette readings for experiments 1 and 2.

Challenge

9 **a** Write a word equation for the reaction taking place in experiments 1 and 2.

....

b In a neutralisation reaction between an acid and an alkali, water is produced. What is the ionic equation for this reaction?

....

c What was the colour change of the indicator observed?

....

d Which of the experiments used the greater volume of hydrochloric acid?

....

e Use your answer to **d** to explain which of the two acid solutions was the more concentrated.

....

....

....

f 10 cm³ of the same sodium hydroxide solution was diluted with an equal volume of water. What is the volume of acid solution **P** required to neutralise the diluted sodium hydroxide solution?

....

....

....

TIP
Neutralisation involves the reaction between an alkali containing excess hydroxide (OH^-) ions and an acid containing excess hydrogen (H^+) ions. When these two ions react they form water which is neutral with a pH of 7. $H^+(aq) + OH^-(aq) \rightarrow H_2O(l)$

> The ionic nature of solutions of acids and bases

KEY WORDS

strong acid: an acid that is completely ionised when dissolved in water – this produces the highest possible concentration of $H^+(aq)$ ions in solution, e.g. hydrochloric acid

weak acid: an acid that is only partially dissociated into ions in water – usually this produces a low concentration of $H^+(aq)$ in the solution, e.g. ethanoic acid

Exercise 11.4

IN THIS EXERCISE YOU WILL:

- describe the relationship between the presence of H^+ and OH^- ions and the pH of a solution

  > show an acid is a proton donor and a base is a proton acceptor

  > investigate the difference between weak and strong acids in terms of ionic dissociation.

Focus

10 The pH scale is the measure of how acidic or alkaline a solution is. It is a measure of whether a solution has an excess of hydrogen or hydroxide ions present. Study Figure 11.4 and complete the diagram by entering the following labels in the correct place:

alkali solution: $OH^- > H^+$

pure water: $H^+ = OH^-$

acid solution: $H^+ > OH^-$

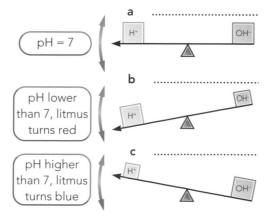

Figure 11.4: The balance of H^+ and OH^- in solutions of different pH.

11 Look at the statements in the table below. Each statement describes either an acid, a base or an alkali. Put ticks in the correct column for each statement.

	Acid	Base	Alkali
A solution of the substance contains an excess of hydroxide (OH⁻) ions.			
A solution of the substance contains an excess of hydrogen (H⁺) ions.			
The substance is a proton acceptor.			
The substance is a proton donor.			

Table 11.4: Statements on the ionic nature of acids and bases.

Practice

12 When describing acids and alkalis, the terms strong and weak have a very specific meaning. Complete the following statements about strong and weak acids by deleting the incorrect words.

a Hydrochloric acid is a **weak** / **strong** acid. Hydrogen chloride gas consists of **covalent** / **ionic** molecules. When they dissolve in water these molecules **partly** / **completely** dissociate into hydrogen and **chlorine** / **chloride** ions, producing as many hydrogen ions in the solution as possible.

b Ethanoic acid is a **weak** / **strong** acid. When it dissolves in water **some** / **all** of the molecules dissociate into ions. The majority of the molecules remain intact. This means that the concentration of hydrogen ions is **more** / **less** than it could be if all the molecules had dissociated into ions.

c Two solutions of hydrochloric acid and ethanoic acid have the same concentration. The hydrochloric acid solution will have the **higher** / **lower** pH value. It has the **higher** / **lower** concentration of hydrogen ions and is the **more** / **less** acidic solution.

> **TIP**
>
> When we talk about acids giving or donating protons, we must remember that a proton is a neutral hydrogen atom minus 1 electron making it positive. This is why a proton in acid–base chemistry is given the symbol H⁺.

Challenge

13 a Complete the following equations for the dissociation into ions in aqueous solution of a weak acid and two strong acids.

   i   ethanoic acid: ....(aq) $\rightleftharpoons$ CH$_3$COO⁻(aq) + ...(aq)

   ii hydrochloric acid: HCl(aq) $\rightarrow$ ....(aq) + ...(aq)

   iii sulfuric acid: ....(aq) $\rightarrow$ ....(aq) + H⁺(aq)

b The equation for ethanoic acid represents an equilibrium. What does the ⇌ sign mean?

....

14 When hydrochloric acid and ethanoic acid react with calcium carbonate, the gas carbon dioxide is formed.

a On the grid provided, draw two sketch graphs to show how the volume of carbon dioxide is formed over time with each acid. You must give the scale for the vertical axis.

- Assume that the acid is the limiting reactant

- Assume that exactly the same amounts of each acid are used for each set of results

- The maximum volume of carbon dioxide formed for each acid is $80\,cm^3$.

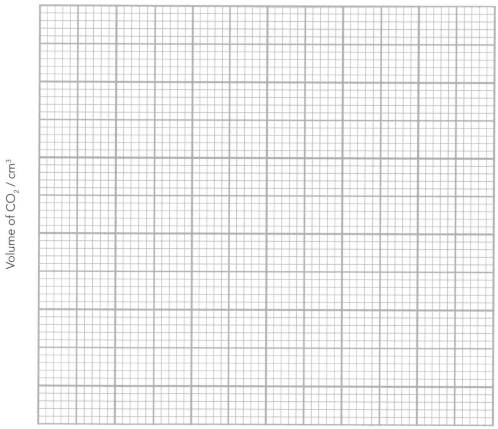

Volume of CO_2 / cm^3

Time / minutes

b Explain the differences between the two graphs you have drawn for each acid.

....

....

....

c Which of the two acid solutions will have the greater electrical conductivity? Explain your answer.

....

....

d When hydrochloric acid is added to ammonia, the following reaction takes place:

$$HCl + NH_3 \rightarrow NH_4^+ + Cl^-$$

How does this equation show that HCl is an acid and NH_3 is a base?

....

....

PEER ASSESSMENT

Exchange your answer to question **14** with your partner.

Assess their graph and answer and make your comments on what they have done in the table.

Aspect of their graph and answer	Comment
Each graph goes up steeply at first and then levels off.	
They have given a scale for the vertical axis.	
Both graphs level off at $80\,cm^3$.	
The graph for HCl goes up more steeply than the graph for ethanoic acid.	
They have mentioned the following points in their explanation of the differences between the two graphs: • the strength of the acids • the concentration of hydrogen ions • the rate of the reaction and how this links to the steepness of the curve.	

Chapter 12

Preparation of salts

> Salt preparation and crystallisation

KEY WORDS

crystallisation: the process of forming crystals from a saturated solution

filtrate: the liquid that passes through the filter paper during filtration

precipitate: an insoluble salt formed during a precipitation reaction

residue: the solid left behind in the filter paper after filtration has taken place

salts: ionic compounds made by the neutralisation of an acid with a base (or alkali), e.g. copper(II) sulfate and potassium nitrate

Exercise 12.1

IN THIS EXERCISE YOU WILL:

- learn more of the characteristic reactions of acids and the types of salt produced by particular acids
- describe the method of preparing crystals of a soluble salt.

Focus

Salts are produced in reactions where the hydrogen of an acid is replaced by metal ions or the ammonium ion. Each acid gives a characteristic family of salts. Sulfuric acid, for instance, always produces sulfates.

1   Complete the following statements for other acids.

   a   Hydrochloric acid always produces a ....

   b   Nitric acid always produces a ....

   c   Phosphoric acid always produces a ....

2   Complete Table 12.1, which summarises the products of various reactions of acids.

Substances reacted together		Salt produced	Other products of the reaction
dilute hydrochloric acid	zinc oxide		
dilute sulfuric acid		copper sulfate	water and carbon dioxide
		magnesium sulfate	water and carbon dioxide
		magnesium chloride	hydrogen
dilute nitric acid	copper oxide		
dilute ethanoic acid		sodium ethanoate	water
	potassium hydroxide	potassium phosphate	

Table 12.1: Reactions that produce different types of salt.

TIP

Although there are many possible combinations of reactions that produce a salt, it is the parent acid that decides the type of salt formed. For example, nitric acid cannot produce any salt other than a nitrate.

Practice

3   Using the words provided, complete the following paragraphs.

acid   anhydrous   carbon dioxide   combined   hydrated   hydrogen

metal   precipitation   sodium   sulfuric   water

All salts are ionic compounds. Salts are produced when an alkali neutralises an

.... In this reaction, the salt is formed when a .... ion or an

ammonium ion from the alkali replaces one or more .... ions of the acid.

Salts can be crystallised from the solution produced by the neutralisation reaction. The salt

crystals formed often contain chemically .... water. These salts are called

.... salts. The salt crystals can be heated to drive off this ....

The salt remaining is said to be ....

Salts can be made by other reactions of acids. Magnesium sulfate can be made by reacting

magnesium carbonate with .... acid. The gas given off is ....

Water is also formed in this reaction.

All .... and potassium salts are soluble in water. Insoluble salts are usually

prepared by ....

Challenge

4 For the following two soluble salts:

- Give the acid and base needed for their preparation.
- Describe briefly how the salt is prepared.

a Magnesium sulfate

....

....

....

....

b Potassium chloride

....

....

....

....

5 Crystals of zinc sulfate can be prepared by reacting dilute sulfuric acid with excess zinc granules.

a Why does the preparation use an excess of the metal?

....

....

b How is the solution of zinc sulfate obtained from the reaction mixture?

....

c The zinc sulfate is prepared from solution by crystallisation. Describe how you would prepare pure dry crystals from the zinc nitrate solution.

....

....

....

....

d Write word and balanced symbol equations for the reaction between the zinc granules and dilute sulfuric acid (include state symbols in your symbol equation).

....

....

6 Crystals of magnesium sulfate ($MgSO_4 \cdot 7H_2O$) can be made by reacting magnesium oxide with dilute sulfuric acid.

a The stages of the preparation following the reaction are listed here, but in an incorrect order. Put the stages in the correct order in which they should be carried out.

A Allow the solution to cool and crystals to form.

B Warm the filtrate until the solution is very concentrated.

C Pour the filtrate into an evaporating basin.

D Wash and dry the crystals.

E Filter the mixture to remove excess magnesium oxide.

F Filter off the crystals.

The correct order is: ....

b Explain why it is necessary to dry the crystals carefully at the end of the preparation rather than heating them strongly.

....

c The formula for hydrated magnesium sulfate is $MgSO_4 \cdot 7H_2O$. What is the term used for this chemically combined water indicated in the formula?

....

> Solubility rules and preparation of insoluble salts

KEY WORDS

limiting reactant: the reactant that is not in excess

precipitation reaction: a reaction in which an insoluble salt is prepared from solutions of two suitable soluble salts

solubility: a measure of how much of a solute dissolves in a solvent at a particular temperature

Exercise 12.2

IN THIS EXERCISE YOU WILL:

- learn which salts are soluble and which salts are insoluble

> work out combinations of reagents required to prepare an insoluble salt

> deduce the formula of an insoluble salt using a precipitation method.

Focus

Insoluble salts can be made using a precipitation reaction.

Figure 12.1 is a Venn diagram showing the solubility of various inorganic compounds.

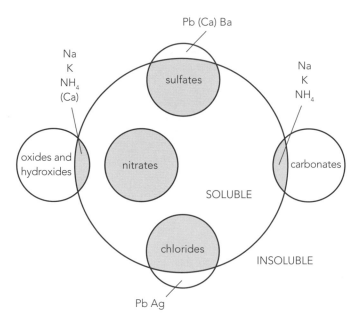

Figure 12.1: A Venn diagram of the solubility of inorganic compounds.

7   Use the information in Figure 12.1 to state whether the following compounds are soluble or insoluble.

    a   sodium sulfate ....

    b   barium sulfate ....

    c   copper(II) hydroxide ....

d   ammonium chloride ....

e   lead(II) iodide ....

f   sodium hydrogen carbonate ....

TIP

It is important to be as familiar as possible with the general solubility rules for salts. The important precipitation tests that are used in chemical analysis will also help you remember the overall patterns of solubility.

When preparing an insoluble salt you need two solutions. Remember that for the metal part of the salt you can use any metal nitrate, and for the acid part you can use the sodium or potassium salt.

Practice

8   For each of the following four insoluble salts (**a–d**), give the two reagents that could be used to prepare them. Give the balanced symbol equation for the reaction taking place in each example.

a   Copper(II) carbonate

Reagents used:

....

Equation:

....

b   Silver iodide

Reagents used:

....

Equation:

....

c   Silver chloride

Reagents used:

....

Equation:

....

d Barium sulfate

Reagents used:

....

Equation:

....

e Choose one of the preparations from **a–d** and write the ionic equation for the reaction.

....

Challenge

9 The precipitation method can be used to find the formula of a salt. In an experiment, $6 \, cm^3$ of a solution of the nitrate of metal X was placed in a narrow test-tube and $1 \, cm^3$ of aqueous sodium phosphate, Na_3PO_4, was added. The precipitate settled and its height was measured. The concentration of both solutions was $1 \, mol/dm^3$.

The experiment was repeated using different volumes of the sodium phosphate solution. The results are shown on the graph (Figure 12.2).

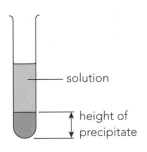
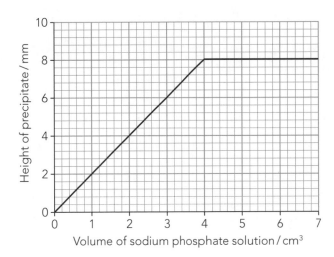

Figure 12.2: Results of a precipitation experiment.

a What is the formula of the phosphate of metal X? Give your reasoning.

....

....

....

b State the ionic equation for the precipitation reaction.

....

c List the three stages by which you would obtain a dry sample of the salt following the precipitation.

....

....

....

PEER ASSESSMENT

With your partner, write down (without your partner seeing) the easiest and most difficult topics in this chapter. If you understood a topic that your partner did not, then explain how you came to understand it.

> Chapter 13
The Periodic Table

> Periodic patterns

KEY WORDS

groups: vertical columns of the Periodic Table containing elements with similar chemical properties; atoms of elements in the same group have the same number of electrons in their outer energy levels

period: a horizontal row of the Periodic Table

periodic property: a property of the elements that shows a repeating pattern when plotted against proton number (Z)

proton number (or atomic number) (Z): the number of protons in the nucleus of an atom

Exercise 13.1

IN THIS EXERCISE YOU WILL:

- consider the organisation of the Periodic Table into groups and periods

- revisit the electronic basis for this arrangement

- recognise the different properties of elements in various groups and periods of the Periodic Table

- identify a periodic or repeating pattern shown by the elements.

Focus

1   Use the words provided to complete the following paragraphs about the Periodic Table. Not all of the words are used, and some of them are used in both the plural and the singular form.

column(s)   electron(s)   group(s)   horizontal   mass

period(s)   proton(s)   row(s)   vertical

The Periodic Table is a way of arranging the elements according to their properties. They are

arranged in order of their .... number. Elements with similar properties are

placed together in .... called ....

Periods are .... of the elements. The table shows trends down the .... and patterns across the ....

The placing of the elements in the table also corresponds to their ....
arrangements (electronic configurations). The number of .... in the outer
.... shell is the same as its .... number in the table. The number of
occupied .... shells of the element is the .... in which it is placed.

Practice

2   Figure 13.1 shows the upper part of the Periodic Table with certain elements named.

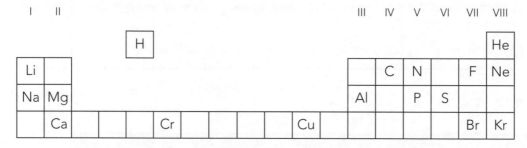

Figure 13.1: A section of the Periodic Table.

Using the elements shown in Figure 13.1, write down the symbols for the elements that answer the following questions.

a   Which two elements are transition metals? ....

b   Which element has just two electrons in the full outer shell of its atom? ....

c   Which element is a red–brown liquid at room temperature and pressure? ....

d   Which element has four electrons in the outer energy level of its atom? ....

e   Which element is a yellow solid at room temperature? ....

f   Which elements are noble gases? ....

g   Which element has compounds that produce blue solutions when they dissolve?

    ....

h   Which element has the electron arrangement 2,8,8,2? ....

i   Which element burns with a brilliant white flame when ignited? ....

Challenge

3   One physical property that shows a repeating pattern when plotted against proton number is the melting point of an element. Figure 13.2 shows the melting points of the elements in Periods 2 and 3 plotted against the proton number of the element.

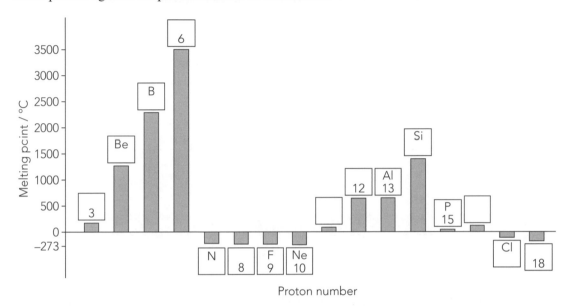

Figure 13.2: The melting points of elements in the second and third periods.

a   Fill in the symbols and proton numbers missing from the boxes in Figure 13.2 (seven symbols and seven proton numbers).

b   Which two elements show the highest melting points?

   .... and ....

c   To which group do these two elements belong? ....

d   Complete the following sentence on this property of the elements.

   When the melting points of elements are plotted against ....

   ...., they show a repeating .... The highest melting points

   are given by the elements of Group number .... and the lowest by the

   .... gases.

> The alkali metals

KEY WORDS

alkali metals: elements in Group I of the Periodic Table; they are the most reactive group of metals

electrical conductor: a substance that conducts electricity but is not chemically changed in the process

insulator: a substance that does not conduct electricity

thermal conductivity: the ability to conduct heat

Exercise 13.2

IN THIS EXERCISE YOU WILL:

- identify certain key properties of the alkali metals and how these properties change as we descend the group

- predict properties of elements from an understanding of the trends within groups or periods of the table.

Focus

4 a Circle the one symbol that represents the most reactive alkali metal.

     C   Ca   Cr   Cs   Cu

  b Circle the one symbol for the element which has the electron arrangement 2,8,1.

     Cs   K   Li   Na   Rb

  c Explain how you can tell from the electronic configuration of the element in **b** that it is in Group I of the Periodic Table.

    ....

  d Circle the words that can be used to describe a Group I element.

          conductor   dense   dull   hard   inert

          insulator   lustrous   reactive   soft

Practice

5   Why are the alkali metals stored under oil?

....

6   A teacher demonstrated the reactions of sodium and potassium with water. The students were asked to write down their observations.

a   Give two similar observations about the reactions of the two metals.

....

....

b   Give one difference between the reactions of the two metals.

....

c   Complete the following symbol equation for the reaction of sodium with water.

.................Na(s) + ...H_2O(l) → ....NaOH(aq) + ...H_2(g)

Challenge

Caesium is an alkali metal. It is in Group I of the Periodic Table.

7   **a**   State two physical properties of caesium.

....

....

b   State the number of electrons in the outer shell of a caesium atom.

....

8 Complete Table 13.1 to estimate the boiling point and atomic radius of caesium. Comment also on the reactivity of potassium and caesium with water. The atomic radius is a measure of the size of the atom.

Group I metal	Density / g per cm³	Radius of metal atom / nm	Boiling point / °C	Reactivity with water
sodium	0.97	0.191	883	floats and fizzes quickly on the surface, disappears gradually and does not burst into flame
potassium	0.86	0.235	760	
rubidium	1.53	0.250	686	reacts instantaneously, fizzes and bursts into flame then spits violently and may explode
caesium	1.88			

Table 13.1: Data on the alkali metals.

SELF-ASSESSMENT

How confident were you at estimating the unknown values that were needed to complete these tables?

Compare your estimations with a partner and discuss the method you used to estimate values for unfamiliar data. Can you work together to come up with a strategy that could be applied to various types of data?

> The halogens

KEY WORD

halogens: elements in Group VII of the Periodic Table – generally the most reactive group of non-metals

Exercise 13.3

IN THIS EXERCISE YOU WILL:

- learn certain key properties of the halogen non-metals and how these properties change as we descend the group
- predict properties of elements from trends within groups or periods
- plot a graph of data for the halogens and interpret information from it.

Focus

9   The halogens are one group of elements in the Periodic Table. Complete the following statements about the halogens by deleting the incorrect words.

   a   The halogens are **metals / non-metals** and their vapours are **coloured / colourless**.

   b   The halogens are **toxic / non-toxic** to humans.

   c   Halogen molecules are each made of **one / two** atoms; they are **monatomic / diatomic**.

   d   Halogens react with **metal / non-metal** elements to form crystalline compounds that are salts.

   e   Halogens can **colour / bleach** vegetable dyes and kill bacteria.

Practice

10 A teacher demonstrated some of the properties of the halogens to their class.

The results are shown in Table 13.2.

Halogen	Reaction with iron wool
Chlorine	When iron wool was lowered into a gas jar, a very exothermic reaction could be seen and dark red solid formed.
Bromine	The iron wool had to be heated at first, but there was a very .... reaction and a .... solid was formed.
Iodine	Lots of heat was needed and a small amount of .... was given out. A .... solid formed.

Table 13.2: The reactions of the halogens with iron wool.

a Complete the gaps in Table 13.2.

b What is the trend in reactivity as we go down (descend) the group?

....

c Balance the following incomplete equation for the reaction of chlorine:

...............$Fe(s)$ + ...$Cl_2(g)$ → ....$FeCl_3(s)$

d Write the balanced symbol equation for the reaction of iron with bromine.

....

Challenge

11 Table 13.3 shows some of the physical properties of the elements of Group VII at atmospheric pressure. These elements are known as the halogens, and the properties show distinct trends as you go down the group.

a Complete Table 13.3 by filling in the spaces. You will estimate the boiling point of bromine in part **c**.

Element	Proton number	Melting point / °C	Boiling point / °C	Colour
fluorine	9	−219	−188	pale yellow
chlorine	17	−101	−34	pale green
bromine	35	−6		
iodine	53	114	185	grey–black
astatine	85	303	337	

Table 13.3: Some properties of the halogens.

b Plot a graph of the melting points and boiling points of the halogens against their proton numbers. Join the points for each property together to produce two separate lines on the graph.

Draw a line across the graph at 20 °C to help you decide which elements are solid, liquid or gas at room temperature and pressure.

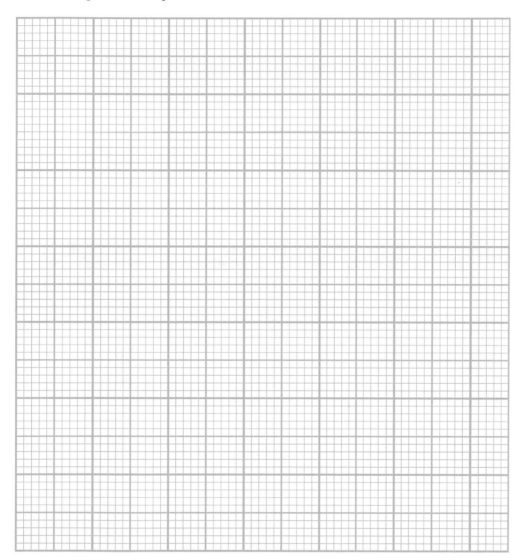

c Use your graph to estimate the boiling point of bromine. State its colour and physical state at room temperature.

Estimated boiling point: .... °C

Colour: ....

Physical state: ....

d Which of the halogens are gases at room temperature and pressure?

....

e   Astatine is very rarely seen. What would you predict to be its physical state and colour at room temperature and pressure?

....

f   What is the trend observed in the melting points of the halogens as you go down the group?

....

> **TIP**
>
> The trends in chemical reactivity run in opposite directions in metallic and non-metallic groups of the table. For metallic groups, reactivity increases down the group. For non-metallic groups, reactivity decreases down the group.

> The transition elements

> **KEY WORDS**
>
> **transition metals (transition elements):** elements from the central region of the Periodic Table – they are hard, strong, dense metals that form compounds that are often coloured

Exercise 13.4

IN THIS EXERCISE YOU WILL:

- review the properties of the transition elements

- distinguish between transition and non-transition elements

- assign properties to the appropriate transition element

- consider the meanings of the Roman numerals used in the naming of transition element compounds

> understand that transition elements can have ions with variable oxidation numbers.

Focus

12 Tick the appropriate boxes to state whether the following statements about the transition elements are true or false.

	True	False
Some transition elements are non-metals.		
Transition elements have high densities.		
Some transition elements make good catalysts.		
Transition elements form only white compounds.		
All transition elements are magnetic.		

Table 13.4: The physical properties of the Noble gases.

Practice

13 For the following statements about metals, give the transition element that can be used as described, or fits the description.

a Used for water pipes ....

b Is part of the catalyst used in car exhausts ....

c Forms a blue sulfate compound ....

d Is a magnetic element ....

e Is the transition element in the compound $KMnO_4$ ....

f Can be used to plate car bumpers ....

g Can be used in jewellery ....

Challenge

14 The transition metals lie in the central region of the Periodic Table.

a What property does the Roman numeral refer to in the name of the oxidising agent, potassium manganate(VII)?

....

b There are two oxides of iron, iron(II) oxide and iron(III) oxide. What common property of transition metals is iron showing in these two oxides?

....

c Give the formulae of the two oxides of iron.

iron(II) oxide: ....

iron(III) oxide: ....

> Non-metals and the noble gases

KEY WORDS

noble gases: elements in Group VIII – a group of stable, very unreactive gases

Exercise 13.5

IN THIS EXERCISE YOU WILL:

- revisit electronic configurations and use them to identify elements

- interpret data on the properties of the noble gases

> examine data on non-metals and use that data to suggest the trends in different properties.

Focus

15 Draw lines from the statements given about non-metals to the electronic configuration of the element described. Note: not all of the electronic configurations are used and more than one arrow can be drawn to an electronic configuration.

Statement

Is an element in the same group as nitrogen
Is a monatomic gas
Is chlorine
Forms the gas SO_2 with an element in the same group
Is a green–yellow gas
Is a brittle yellow solid

Electronic configuration

2,8,2
2,8,5
2,8,8
2,8,6
2,8,7

Practice

16 The noble gases (Group VIII) are unreactive, monatomic gases. Table 13.5 shows data on some members of this group of gases.

Noble gas	Density g/dm³	Atomic number	Period	Electronic configuration
Helium	0.18	2	1	.....
Neon	0.90	10	2	2,8
Argon	1.78	18		2,8,.....
Krypton	3.75	36		2,8,18,8
Xenon	5.89	54	5	2,8,18,18,8

Table 13.5: Data on some of the noble gases.

Note that the density of air is 1.28 g/dm³.

a Complete the missing period numbers and electronic configurations in Table 13.5.

b What is the relationship between the period an element is in and the number of occupied shells (energy levels) in an atom?

....

c Explain why helium is a good gas for balloons.

....

....

d If a balloon is filled with argon, will it fall to the ground or rise into the air? Explain your answer.

....

....

TIP

The stability of the noble gas configuration of electrons is very important in understanding both ionic and covalent chemical bonding. It is usually the electronic configuration of their nearest noble gas that atoms are trying to achieve when they make bonds.

> ## Challenge

17 Elements within a group tend to show clear trends in their physical properties as you go down a group. The following solid elements in Group VI show this. Use the following values to complete Table 13.6.

685   4.79   0.198   450   0.221

Name of element	sulfur	selenium	tellurium
Density / g per cm³	2.07		6.24
Melting point / °C	115	221	
Boiling point / °C	445		988
Ionic radius / nm	0.184		

Table 13.6: Properties of some elements in Group VI.

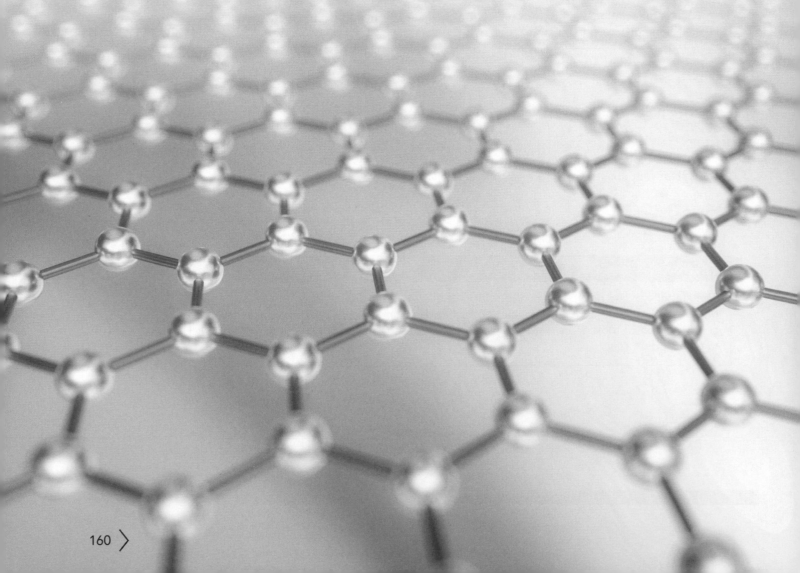

> Chapter 14

Metallic elements and alloys

> Metals and alloys

KEY WORDS

ductile: a word used to describe the property that metals can be drawn out and stretched into wires

malleable: a word used to describe the property that metals can be bent and beaten into sheets

sonorous: a word to describe a metallic substance that rings like a bell when hit with a hammer

---

Exercise 14.1

IN THIS EXERCISE YOU WILL:

- investigate the general physical properties of metals and non-metals

- show how the chemical and physical properties of metals support the way in which they are used

- describe the chemical reaction of certain metals with water and dilute acids.

Focus

Metals have several physical properties in common. Most metals show these properties and are the reason why metals are so useful.

1 The physical properties shared by metals are summarised in Figure 14.1. Complete Figure 14.1 by filling in the missing words or phrases.

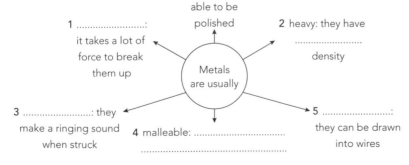

Figure 14.1: Physical properties of metals.

2 Now complete Table 14.1. Use the following words or phrases to complete the first two columns. Then identify a use and base it on that property.

high density   they are ductile   electrical conductivity   malleability

strength   they are sonorous   they transfer heat well

Description of physical property	Name for this property	Use that depends on this property
They can be moulded or bent into shape.		
	thermal conductivity	
They can be drawn into wires.		
They conduct electricity.		
They are heavy for their volume.		
They can bear weight and are not broken easily.		
They make a ringing sound when struck by a hammer.		

Table 14.1: The properties and uses of metals.

3 The physical properties of non-metals tend to be the opposite of those of metals. Complete the following sentences by stating the general property of non-metals in each case.

a Metals show good electrical conductivity whereas non-metals are …

....

b Metals are malleable and ductile but non-metals are …

....

c Metals are good conductors of heat but most non-metals are …

....

d Metals are usually grey in colour and can be polished whereas non-metals are …

....

Practice

4   Table 14.2 shows some properties of a selection of pure metals.

Metal	Relative abundance in Earth's crust	Cost of extraction	Density	Strength	Melting point / °C	Electrical conductivity relative to iron
iron	2nd	low	high	high	1535	1.0
titanium	7th	very high	low	high	1660	0.2
aluminium	1st	high	low	medium	660	3.5
zinc	19th	low	high	low	419	1.7
copper	20th	low	high	medium	1083	6.0
tin	40th	low	high	low	231	0.9
lead	30th	low	very high	low	327	0.5

Table 14.2: The properties of certain metals.

Use information from the table to answer the following questions.

a   Why is aluminium used for overhead power cables?

   ....

b   What advantage does the low density of aluminium give to the use of this metal in overhead power cables?

   ....

c   Why is copper used instead of aluminium in wiring in the home?

   ....

d   Why is titanium a good metal to use for jet aircraft and Formula 1 racing cars?

   ....

   ....

Challenge

5 A student carried out some experiments on the reactivity of some common metals.

 a They first placed pieces of four different metals into test-tubes of dilute hydrochloric acid.

 Figure 14.2 shows the progress of the reactions after a few minutes. Use the information presented to put the metals into order of decreasing reactivity.

 Explain why you have put the metals in this order.

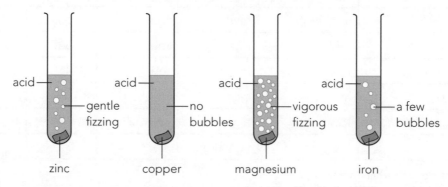

Figure 14.2: The progress of the reactions of four metals with acid.

....

....

....

....

 b Name the gas being given off in all the reactions.

....

 c Write the word equation for the reaction between zinc and hydrochloric acid.

....

6 The student was then given further samples of three metals, labelled A, B and C. These were first put into cold water to see if there was any reaction. If no reaction occurred, then the sample was tested to see if it reacted with steam. The results were recorded in Table 14.3.

Metal sample	Reaction with cold water	Reaction with steam
A	No reaction.	No reaction.
B	Reacted very vigorously, hydrogen gas produced.	
C	No reaction.	Reacted strongly. Metal coated with white solid. Hydrogen gas produced.

Table 14.3: The reactions of three metals with water and steam.

a Metal C was magnesium. Name the white solid produced in the reaction.

....

b One of the other metals was sodium. Suggest whether sodium was metal A or metal B and name the solution that remained after the reaction was complete in this case.

....

c Put the three metals in order of increasing reactivity.

....

d Which of these metals must be kept under oil to prevent it from reacting with the oxygen in the air?

....

e Metal C burns in air to produce a white compound. What is the name and formula of this compound?

....

SELF-ASSESSMENT

It is important that you can review a series of experiments on different metals and predict an order of reactivity from the results. How confident did you feel when answering the questions here and listing the metals in the required order? Are you familiar with the language and terms used?

〉 Alloys and their uses

KEY WORDS

alloys: mixtures of elements (usually metals) designed to have the properties useful for a particular purpose, e.g. solder (an alloy of tin and lead) has a low melting point

brass: an alloy of copper and zinc; this alloy is hard

stainless steel: an alloy of iron that resists corrosion; this steel contains a significant proportion of chromium which results in the alloy being resistant to rusting

Exercise 14.2

IN THIS EXERCISE YOU WILL:

- investigate the nature of alloys and explore how the properties of alloys are linked to their use

> explain how the different sized atoms in the structure of an alloy make the alloy stronger or harder than the pure metals.

Focus

7 Metals and their alloys play a big part in our everyday lives. Some metals are very familiar to us. Link the properties (**a–f**) on the left with the metals (**i–vi**) on the right.

a	an alloy that looks like gold
b	a metal that is liquid at room temperature
c	an alloy of iron that does not rust
d	a metal with a low density that resists corrosion
e	a very unreactive precious metal
f	a metal with good electrical conductivity used in wiring

i	gold
ii	aluminium
iii	brass
iv	copper
v	stainless steel
vi	mercury

Practice

8 Table 14.4 describes the composition and usefulness of some alloys. Complete Table 14.4 by filling in the gaps.

Alloy	Composition	Use	Useful property
mild steel	iron: >99.75% carbon: <0.25%	....	....
stainless steel	iron: 74% ....: 18% nickel: 8%	........................, surgical instruments, ...	resistant to corrosion (does not rust easily)
brass	copper: 70% ....: 30%	.... instruments, ornaments	'gold' colour, harder than copper
bronze	copper: 95% ....: 5%	statues, church bells	hard, does not ....
aerospace aluminium	aluminium: 90.25% zinc: 6% magnesium: 2.5% copper: 1.25%	aircraft construction	....
solder	tin: 60% lead: 40%	....	low melting point
tungsten steel	iron: 95% tungsten: 5%	cutting edges of drill bits	....

Table 14.4: The composition and usefulness of some alloys.

> **TIP**
>
> Alloys are usually harder and stronger than the parent metals themselves. However, there can also be specific improvements to their other properties.

Challenge

9   Alloys have different properties from the metals they are made from. They are usually harder and stronger, more resistant to corrosion, and have lower melting points.

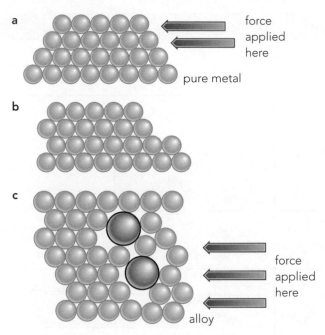

Figure 14.3 a and b: The effects of applying a force to a pure metal. **c:** The effects of applying a force to an alloy.

a   Using information from Figure 14.3a and b, explain why metals can be shaped in this way (i.e. why are metals malleable)?

   ....

   ....

b   Solder, which is melted to join together electrical components on circuit boards, is a mixture of tin and lead. Suggest why we use solder for this purpose, rather than the pure metals.

   ....

   ....

c   Stainless steel is a form of steel made by alloying iron with which two other metals to make it resistant to corrosion (rusting)? Which block of the Periodic Table do these two metals come from?

   ....

d   Figure 14.3c represents the structure of an alloy of the metal. Explain how the alloy is stronger than the metals from which it is made.

   ....

e   Commercial aluminium used in construction and engineering is 99.5% pure. This aluminium contains some iron and silicon. Explain why industry prefers to use this form of aluminium rather than pure aluminium.

....

....

f   Copper used in electrical circuits must be very pure. Sketch a diagram of the metallic bonding in copper. Use your diagram to explain how the presence of impurities would lower the electrical conductivity of the copper.

....

....

g   Brass is an alloy of copper and zinc. It is used to make brass musical instruments and to make electrical connectors and plugs.

There are two main types of brass: 60:40 and 70:30 copper to zinc. The larger the amount of zinc, the harder and stronger the alloy is. Suggest which alloy is used for each of these purposes. Give a reason for your answers.

i   Cu60:Zn40

....

....

ii   Cu70:Zn30

....

....

TIP

The ability to draw detailed diagrams of metallic bonding and the layered structure of pure metals and alloys is important for explaining the electrical conductivity of metals and the strength of alloys.

Chapter 15

Reactivity of metals

> Reactions of metals with water and acid

KEY WORDS

reactivity series of metals: an order of reactivity, giving the most reactive metal first, based on results from a range of experiments involving metals reacting with oxygen, water, dilute hydrochloric acid and metal salt solutions

---

Exercise 15.1

IN THIS EXERCISE YOU WILL:

- consider how the reactivity of metals changes within a group of the Periodic Table

- investigate how the reactions of metals with water and steam show which metals are more reactive than others.

Focus

In the Periodic Table, elements are arranged in vertical columns known as groups. Each group contains elements with similar chemical properties. Within a group there are trends in both chemical reactivity and physical properties.

1   Two of the elements in Group I (the alkali metals) of the table are sodium and potassium. When they are added to cold water there is a strong reaction in both cases. If a few drops of thymolphthalein solution are added to the water, then it turns blue as the metal reacts.

    a   Explain why these metals are part of a group called the alkali metals.

    ....

    ....

    b   Give the electronic configurations of sodium and potassium.

    sodium: ....

    potassium: ....

    c   What is the feature of the electronic configurations of sodium and potassium that places them in Group I of the Periodic Table?

    ....

d When sodium is added to water it melts and skids over the surface with fizzing caused by the hydrogen gas given off. Potassium reacts with a burst of energy which causes the hydrogen to burn with a purple flame. Which of these metals is the more reactive when added to cold water?

....

e Write a word equation for the reaction of potassium with water.

....

f Complete the balanced symbol equation for the reaction between potassium and water by inserting the missing formulae and balancing numbers in the following:

..........................K(s) + ...(l) $\rightarrow$ 2KOH(aq) + ...(g)

Practice

2 a What observation do you see when a piece of sodium is added to water that suggests the reaction is exothermic?

....

b If the sodium is held in place on the water the hydrogen bursts into flame. What colour is the flame, and why is it that colour?

....

....

c Magnesium is a metal in Group II of the Periodic Table. Metals in this group are less reactive than the alkali metals. Magnesium only reacts very slowly with cold water but does react strongly when heated in steam. Write the word and balanced symbol equations for the reaction between magnesium and steam.

....

....

Challenge

3 Magnesium, calcium, strontium and barium are metals in Group II of the Periodic Table, and details of some properties of these metals are given in Table 15.1. The atomic radius of a metal atom is a measure of the size of that atom.

a State the number of electrons in the outer shell of an atom of any of these metals.

....

b Complete Table 15.1 by commenting on the reactivity of strontium with water and steam.

Group II metal	Density / g per cm³	Radius of metal atom / nm	Boiling point / °C	Reactivity with water and steam
magnesium	1.74	0.173	1090	reacts very slowly with cold water, but reacts strongly with steam
calcium	1.54	0.231	1484	reacts strongly with cold water, unsafe to react with steam
strontium	2.64	0.249	1377	
barium	3.62	0.268	1845	reacts strongly with cold water, unsafe to react with steam

Table 15.1: Group II metals.

c What trend do you see in atomic size as you descend Group II?

....

d Consider the values for the density and boiling point of these metals and suggest which metal shows values that do not fit the general trend as you descend the group.

....

e Write the word and balanced symbol equations for the reaction of calcium with water, include state symbols in the balanced equation.

....

....

f What is the trend in reactivity with water and steam that is seen when descending a group of metals?

....

> **TIP**
>
> Remember that metals that react with cold water produce the metal hydroxide as a product. Those metals that only react with steam produce the metal oxide.

> The reactivity series

KEY WORDS

displacement reaction: a reaction in which a more reactive element displaces a less reactive element from a solution of its salt

Exercise 15.2

IN THIS EXERCISE YOU WILL:

- describe how the reactivity of metals changes within a group of the Periodic Table

- show how the results from experiments contribute to the organisation of the reactivity series

> explain how the ability of metals to form positive ions relates to a series of metal displacement reactions.

Focus

4   Complete the following paragraph about the reactivity of metals using the words provided.

>   acids   alkaline   cold   hydrogen   lower   oxide   red   steam

When metals react with .... water, the products are a metal hydroxide and

.... The hydroxides formed are .... and they will turn

.... litmus blue. Some metals do not react with cold water but do with

.... The products in this reaction are the metal .... and hydrogen.

Copper does not react with water or with dilute .... This is because it is

.... in the reactivity series than hydrogen.

Using the results of various different types of chemical reaction, the metals can be arranged into the reactivity series.

5   a   Zinc does not react with cold water, but it does react with steam to give zinc oxide and a gas. Write the word equation for the reaction between zinc and steam.

....

b   Choose one metal from the reactivity series that will not react with steam.

....

c   Choose one metal (other than zinc) from the reactivity series that will safely react with dilute sulfuric acid.

....

Practice

6   When a metal is added to a solution of the salt of a less reactive metal, a displacement reaction takes place. The equations for two different examples are:

$Fe(s) + CuSO_4(aq) \rightarrow Cu(s) + FeSO_4(aq)$

zinc + copper sulfate $\rightarrow$ copper + zinc sulfate

The energy change involved in these reactions can be measured by adding 5 g of metal powder to 50 cm³ of 0.5 mol/dm³ copper(II) sulfate solution in a polystyrene cup. The temperature of the solution is taken before adding the metal. The powder is then added, the reaction mixture is stirred continuously, and temperatures are taken every 30 seconds for three minutes.

A student took the following readings when carrying out this experiment.

Time / minutes	0.0	0.5	1.0	1.5	2.0	2.5	3.0
Experiment 1 (zinc) temperature / °C	21	48	62	71	75	72	70
Experiment 2 (iron) temperature / °C	21	25	32	38	41	43	44

Table 15.2: Data on the thermochemistry of metal displacement reactions.

a   Plot two graphs on the grid provided and label each with the name of the metal.

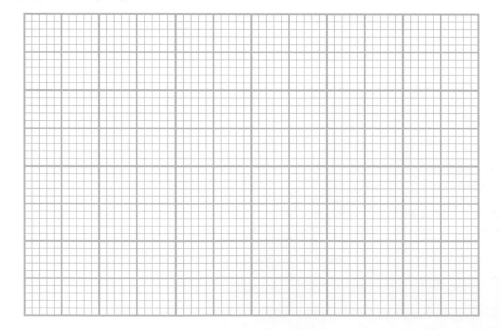

> **TIP**
>
> When you draw a graph, the scales for the axes should use more than half of the graph grid in both directions. Also, use appropriate scales; for example, use 2 cm on the graph grid to represent 10, 20 or 50 units of the variable. Note that the scale on either axis does not necessarily have to begin at zero.

> **SELF-ASSESSMENT**
>
> Graphs need to be accurately drawn so that experimental results can be clearly interpreted. Have you chosen a suitable scale for each axis so that the values can be easily plotted? Have you drawn suitable lines of best fit using the points plotted?
>
> How did your background knowledge of displacement reactions help you to decide the best lines to draw for zinc and iron?

b From your graphs, comment on which reaction gave the steepest initial increase in temperature.

....

....

c Why do the temperatures stop rising after 2 or 2.5 minutes?

....

....

d Write the word equation for the first reaction and the balanced symbol equation for the second reaction.

....

....

e Which metal, iron or zinc, produced the larger temperature rise? Suggest why this metal gave the larger temperature rise.

....

....

f Comment on whether this experiment is a 'fair test' giving a good indication as to which of zinc or iron is the more reactive metal. Explain your answer.

....

....

....

....

> TIP
>
> When carrying out an experiment that is a 'fair test' you should make sure that everything is the same except the thing you are testing. Only the independent variable (e.g. time) has been allowed to affect the dependent variable.

Challenge

7   In each of the experiments shown in Table 15.3, a piece of metal is placed in a solution of a metal salt.

   a   Complete the table of observations.

<table>
<thead>
<tr><th colspan="2"></th><th>zinc
tin(II) chloride solution</th><th>zinc
copper(II) sulfate solution</th><th>tin
copper(II) sulfate solution</th><th>silver
copper(II) sulfate solution</th><th>copper
silver nitrate solution</th></tr>
</thead>
<tbody>
<tr><td rowspan="2">At start</td><td>Colour of metal</td><td>grey</td><td></td><td>silver coloured</td><td>silver coloured</td><td></td></tr>
<tr><td>Colour of solution</td><td>colourless</td><td></td><td>blue</td><td>blue</td><td>colourless</td></tr>
<tr><td rowspan="2">At finish</td><td>Colour of metal</td><td>coated with silver-coloured crystals</td><td></td><td>coated with brown solid</td><td>silver coloured</td><td>coated with silver-coloured crystals</td></tr>
<tr><td>Colour of solution</td><td>colourless</td><td></td><td>colourless</td><td>blue</td><td></td></tr>
</tbody>
</table>

Table 15.3: The results of several metal displacement reactions.

   b   Use these results to place the metals copper, silver, tin and zinc in order of reactivity (putting the most reactive metal first).

.... > .... > .... > ....

The box contains some familiar and unfamiliar metals, placed in order of reactivity. Asterisks (*) are given next to those elements that are unfamiliar and the common oxidation states are provided for the unfamiliar elements.

barium*	Ba (+2)	chromium*	Cr (+2),(+3),(+6)
lanthanum*	La (+3)	iron	
aluminium		copper	
zinc		palladium*	Pd (+2)

c Explain which of the following two equations is correct for the two metals, lanthanum and aluminium.

$$2La(s) + Al_2(SO_4)(aq) \rightarrow 2Al(s) + La_2(SO_4)_3(aq)$$

$$2Al(s) + La_2(SO_4)_3(aq) \rightarrow 2La(s) + Al_2(SO_4)_3(aq)$$

....

....

....

d To which block of elements in the Periodic Table would you place iron and chromium?

....

e Apart from variable oxidation numbers, give two other properties of these metals and their compounds that set them apart from other metals.

....

....

f Aluminium can show an apparently lower reactivity than it actually possesses. Explain why this is the case.

....

....

....

TIP

This question asks you to apply your knowledge of certain metals to other metals you are unfamiliar with. You should be prepared to be able to do this and not be put off by such questions. The ability to apply your knowledge of principles and concepts to a new situation is an important part of learning.

8 The reactivity of metals is related directly to the ease with which they form positive ions. The electrons lost from the metal atoms are those in the outer energy level (the valency electrons). The ease of loss of the valency electrons depends on:

- how far the outer shell is from the nucleus of the atom

- the number of inner shells of electrons there are

- the number of protons in the nucleus.

Considering these factors, explain why:

a Magnesium is less reactive than sodium even though its outer electrons are in the same energy level.

....

....

....

b Potassium is more reactive than sodium.

....

....

....

> Chapter 16

Extraction and corrosion of metals

> Metal extraction and reactivity

KEY WORD

ore: a naturally occurring mineral from which a metal can be extracted

Exercise 16.1

IN THIS EXERCISE YOU WILL:

- describe how reactivity affects the way in which metals are extracted

- investigate how reduction can be used in the extraction of metals.

Focus

1   Table 16.1 shows the order of reactivity of some metals in the reactivity series. The position of carbon is also shown.

Metal	Reactivity	Method of extraction	Energy needed to extract the metal	Cost of extracting the metal
sodium				
calcium				
magnesium				
aluminium				
carbon				
zinc				
lead				
copper				
silver				
gold				

Table 16.1: The reactivity of metals and their extraction.

a   Draw an arrow in the second column of the table showing the increasing reactivity of the metals.

b   Label the third column in the table with either 'reduction by heating with carbon' or 'extraction by electrolysis' in the appropriate spaces.

c   Draw arrows in the fourth and fifth columns to show the trends in the energy required and the cost of extraction (they should be drawn from 'most' to 'least' in both cases).

Practice

2   Gold can be found native in the ground as the metal itself. Which other elements can be found as the uncombined metal in the ground?

....

3   Which is the most reactive metal that can be extracted from its oxide by using carbon?

....

4   Could hydrogen be used to extract this metal from its ore? Explain your answer.

....

....

5 The main ore of sodium is rock salt (sodium chloride). Explain how sodium can be obtained from this ore.

....

....

Challenge

6 Aluminium used to be regarded as a rare and expensive metal as it was very difficult to extract.

a Before the electrolysis method was invented, it was extracted by reduction of aluminium chloride by sodium. Why is sodium a good reducing agent that can be used to extract aluminium from its chloride?

....

b Complete the following symbol and ionic equations showing the displacement of aluminium from its chloride using sodium.

i ....Na(s) + $AlCl_3$(s) → ....NaCl(s) + Al(s)

ii ....Na(s) + ...(s) → ....Na^+(s) + Al(s)

7 Aluminium can itself be used as a reducing agent to extract small amounts of iron from iron(III) oxide. The reaction gives out a large amount of thermal energy.

a What name is given to reactions that give out thermal energy to the surroundings?

....

b Write the word and balanced symbol equations for the reaction.

....

....

c Use the information in this question to put the metals aluminium, iron and sodium in order of increasing reactivity.

....

> The extraction of iron and the blast furnace

KEY WORDS

blast furnace: a furnace for extracting metals (particularly iron) by reduction with carbon that uses hot air blasted in at the base of the furnace to raise the temperature

limestone: a form of calcium carbonate ($CaCO_3$)

slag: a molten mixture of impurities, mainly calcium silicate, formed in the blast furnace

Exercise 16.2

IN THIS EXERCISE YOU WILL:

- show how the blast furnace can be used to extract iron and other metals from their ores

- describe the details of the blast furnace process for the extraction of iron.

Focus

Iron and zinc are both extracted from their oxides using a blast furnace.

8   Figure 16.1 shows a diagram of the blast furnace for extracting iron. A, B, C, D and E show where various important substances enter or leave the furnace.

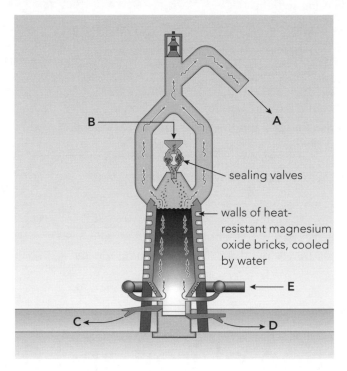

Figure 16.1: The blast furnace for extraction of iron.

Choose from A to E where the following occur:

a   Hot air enters the furnace: ....

b   Molten slag leaves the furnace: ....

c   The waste gases leave the furnace to be recycled: ....

d   Iron ore, coke and limestone are fed into the furnace: ....

e   Molten iron leaves the furnace: ....

9   Why is the furnace used to extract iron called a blast furnace?

....

Practice

10   In the blast furnace, iron is extracted from its ore. Answer the following questions on the chemistry of this process.

a   What is the name of the main ore of iron?

....

b   Where, in the furnace, is iron reduced?

....

c   What gas is the actual reducing agent in the furnace?

....

d   Write the word equation for the reduction reaction that converts iron ore into iron in the furnace.

....

e   Why does iron collect at the bottom of the furnace?

....

Challenge

11   Write the balanced symbol equation for:

a   the reduction reaction converting iron ore into iron in the furnace (include state symbols in your symbol equation)

....

....

b   the thermal decomposition of limestone to lime.

....

....

12   Slag (calcium silicate) is a salt produced by a neutralisation reaction. What are the acid and base which react?

a   The acid is: ....

b   The base is: ....

c   Write the balanced symbol equation for this reaction between acidic and basic oxides.

....

13 Zinc can also be extracted from zinc oxide by carbon reduction in a blast furnace.

 a Zinc boils at 907 °C. Why is zinc collected as a liquid at the top of the furnace?

 ....

 ....

 ....

 b The liquid iron collected at the bottom of its furnace is impure. Why is the liquid zinc, which is condensed at the top of its furnace, pure?

 ....

 ....

 ....

TIP

The addition of limestone to the furnace is quite specific to the extraction of iron. Its role in providing calcium oxide to react with the silica that contaminates the iron ore is vital. Otherwise the glass that would form in the furnace from the heated silica would stop the furnace working.

> The extraction of aluminium

Exercise 16.3

IN THIS EXERCISE YOU WILL:

- describe the ionic nature of the major mineral ore of aluminium and the fact that electrolysis must be used to extract the metal

- show how aluminium is extracted from aluminium oxide by electrolysis

- describe the details of the electrolytic extraction of aluminium.

Focus

14 Because of its high reactivity, aluminium must be extracted by electrolysis.

a The electrolyte is molten aluminium oxide. What is the main ore of aluminium from which aluminium oxide is purified?

....

b Give the formula of aluminium oxide and state the ions present in the compound.

....

c Why must the electrolyte be molten for electrolysis to occur?

....

d State the name of the products formed at the anode and cathode during this electrolysis.

i At the anode: ....

ii At the cathode: ....

e State one use of aluminium.

....

Practice

15 Figure 16.2 shows a diagram of the electrolytic cell used in the extraction of aluminium.

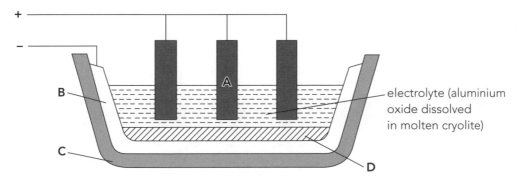

Figure 16.2: The electrolytic cell for extracting aluminium.

a Which letter represents the cathode? ....

b Which letter represents the anode? ....

c What do the other two letters represent in the diagram?

....

....

d What is the purpose of the cryolite?

....

....

e Why do the anodes have to be renewed periodically?

....

f Complete the ionic half-equations for the reactions at the electrodes under the conditions present in the cell.

$$Al^{3+}(l) + ...e^- \rightarrow Al(l)$$

$$....O^{2-}(....) \rightarrow O_2(....) + ...e^-$$

Challenge

16 Aluminium ore is a mixture of aluminium oxide (Al_2O_3) and iron(III) oxide (Fe_2O_3). Sodium hydroxide is added to the mixture during the refining process. Aluminium oxide dissolves but iron(III) oxide does not.

a Explain why this happens by considering the types of oxide involved.

....

....

b Aluminium hydroxide is recovered from the mixture and heated.

$$2Al(OH)_3 \rightarrow Al_2O_3 + 3H_2O$$

What type of reaction is this? Circle the correct answer.

decomposition   neutralisation   oxidation   reduction

PEER ASSESSMENT

The methods of extraction of iron and aluminium both depend on a process of reduction. However, the reactions involved show the different definitions of reduction. Discuss the definitions of oxidation and reduction with other members of your group and test each other on these methods of extraction and other examples of redox reactions.

> Rusting

KEY WORDS

galvanising: the protection of iron and steel objects by coating with a layer of zinc

rusting: the corrosion of iron and steel to form rust (hydrated iron(III) oxide)

sacrificial protection: a method of rust protection involving the attachment of blocks of a metal more reactive than iron to a structure; this metal is corroded rather than the iron or steel structure

Exercise 16.4

IN THIS EXERCISE YOU WILL:

* investigate the factors involved in the rusting of iron

* consider some of the different methods used to prevent rusting.

Focus

17 Figure 16.3 shows an experiment to investigate the conditions needed for iron to rust.

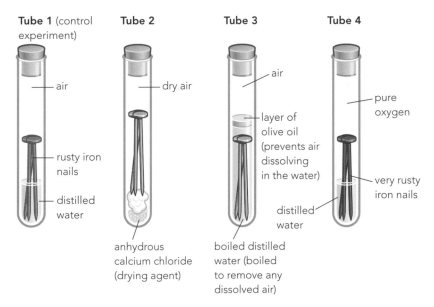

Figure 16.3: Experiment on the rusting of iron.

a What was the purpose of the anhydrous calcium chloride in the second tube?

....

b Why was boiled distilled water used in tube 3?

....

c What was the purpose of the oil layer in tube 3?

....

d In which tube did the iron rust most?

....

e What could have been added to the water to make the nails rust even more than they did in this tube?

....

18 a In addition to the iron or steel object, what two substances need to be present for rusting to occur?

....

b Barrier methods can be used to prevent rusting. Give two examples of such barrier methods that exclude the substances just mentioned in part **a**.

....

....

〉 Practice

19 Food cans (Figure 16.4) are usually made from steel. Steel can corrode, and this limits the length of time for which food can be stored.

Figure 16.4: A typical food can.

The outside can be coated with a substance to act as a barrier to air and water. The inside presents more of a problem. Many of the substances which could be used may be toxic if they combine with the food.

Air and water cannot reach the food inside the can, but many types of food contain acids which can attack the steel of the can. One solution is to coat the steel can with another metal. Some possible metals (together with iron) are listed in order of reactivity:

(**most reactive**) aluminium > zinc > iron > tin > lead (**least reactive**)

a Why might rust on the outside of the can affect the food?

....

....

b Why would zinc be a good metal for the outside of the can?

....

....

c Why would zinc be a bad choice for the inside of the can?

....

....

d Why would tin be a good choice for the inside of the can?

....

....

Challenge

20 Tin is the metal now used to coat both the inside and outside of food cans.

a The first cans used lead but this was discontinued even though lead is less reactive than tin. Suggest why.

....

....

b Rapid corrosion can sometimes happen when cans of food are damaged or dented. Suggest why damaging the layer of tin might cause this to happen.

....

....

21 Aluminium cans are used for drinks. Suggest reasons why they are not often used for food.

....

....

22 Coating an iron or steel object with zinc is a useful barrier method to prevent rusting.

a What name is given to coating an object with zinc?

....

b Coating with zinc continues to prevent rusting even if the protective layer is scratched or broken. Why does this happen?

....

....

23 Protection from rusting using blocks of a metal that is more reactive than iron is known as sacrificial protection. Figure 16.5 shows the use of zinc blocks attached to the hull of a yacht to prevent rusting.

Figure 16.5: A large motor yacht in dry dock showing propellers and zinc blocks attached to the hull.

Sacrificial protection requires blocks of a metal higher in the reactivity series than iron, as such metals react to form cations more readily than iron.

a   Name another metal that is often used for sacrificial protection.

    ....

b   Complete the following half equation showing the formation of zinc ions during sacrificial protection.

$$Zn(....) \rightarrow Zn^{2+}(....) + ...e^-$$

TIP
In choosing the metal other than zinc which could be used for sacrificial protection, think carefully about the conditions the blocks will be under and what, therefore, would be an appropriate metal to use.

> Chapter 17

Chemistry of our environment

> Air quality

KEY WORDS

acid rain: rain that has been made more acidic than normal by the presence of dissolved pollutants such as sulfur dioxide (SO2) and oxides of nitrogen (nitrogen oxides, (NOx)

atmosphere: the layer of air and water vapour surrounding the Earth

catalytic converter: a device for converting polluting exhaust gases from cars into less dangerous emissions

clean dry air: containing no water vapour and only the gases which are always present in the air

climate change: changes in weather patterns brought about by global warming

complete combustion: a type of combustion reaction in which a fuel is burned in a plentiful supply of oxygen; the complete combustion of hydrocarbon fuels produces only carbon dioxide and water

desulfurisation: an industrial process for removing contaminating sulfur from fossil fuels such as petrol (gasoline) or diesel

fossil fuels: fuels, such as coal, oil and natural gas, formed underground over geological periods of time from the remains of plants and animals

global warming: a long-term increase in the average temperature of the Earth's surface, which may be caused in part by human activities

particulates: very tiny solid particles produced during the combustion of fuels

pollutants: substances, often harmful, which are added to another substance

Exercise 17.1

IN THIS EXERCISE YOU WILL:

- identify the names and formulae of gases found in the atmosphere, and describe the composition of clean dry air

- describe which of the atmospheric gases are pollutants and investigate the sources of these pollutants

- consider the problems caused by different air pollutants and the methods of reducing the levels of these pollutants.

Focus

1 **a** Find the names of eight gases in this wordsearch puzzle and enter their names into Table 17.1. Names may be present in any direction, including diagonally.

```
A  R  G  L  A  N  S  H  I  F  O  M  T  I  L  E
M  C  H  O  R  I  C  P  R  E  U  M  A  S  D  B
O  U  T  T  I  C  R  H  N  O  Y  L  O  I  S  F
T  H  I  S  U  L  F  U  R  D  I  O  X  I  D  E
A  L  B  O  R  I  T  A  S  K  R  O  Y  Z  P  L
S  V  R  M  J  P  H  G  T  I  N  T  G  A  Q  U
Q  K  L  C  F  E  G  S  E  O  N  L  E  C  D  P
N  R  E  N  A  H  T  E  M  S  O  U  N  P  Y  F
H  Y  D  R  O  G  E  N  L  E  G  N  P  Z  L  R
B  E  N  X  R  U  O  P  A  V  R  E  T  A  W  A
W  R  O  M  I  B  A  R  T  S  A  O  T  F  A  M
F  N  P  Q  R  V  P  E  S  L  P  R  M  N  E  D
F  R  K  A  E  A  L  M  S  P  V  Y  L  P  A  O
P  S  C  A  R  B  O  N  D  I  O  X  I  D  E  M
```

Formula	Name of gas	Found in clean dry air	Considered a pollutant
Ar			
CO_2			
CO			
H_2			
CH_4			
N_2			
NO_2			
O_2			
SO_2			
H_2O			

Table 17.1: Gases in the wordsearch puzzle.

b   Which of the gases that you found in the wordsearch is not normally found in clean dry air?

....

c   Which of the gases that you found in the wordsearch is the most abundant gas in clean dry air? What is the approximate percentage of this gas in clean dry air?

Gas: ....

Percentage: ....

d   Add the names of the two gases not included in the wordsearch to Table 17.1.

....and...

e   Which two gases in the completed Table 17.1 are unreactive?

....and...

f   Complete the final two columns of Table 17.1 by putting a tick in the correct columns.

g   Which gas in Table 17.1 is found in the atmosphere in two different physical states?

....

> **TIP**
>
> Clean dry air does not contain any water vapour and around 99% of clean dry air is composed of just two gases.

Practice

2   a   In the grid, link each gas with its environmental sources and with the adverse effect(s) which it causes by drawing a line between them. The first gas (methane) has been done for you.

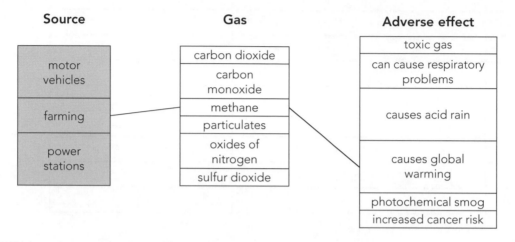

Source	Gas	Adverse effect
motor vehicles	carbon dioxide	toxic gas
	carbon monoxide	can cause respiratory problems
farming	methane	causes acid rain
	particulates	
power stations	oxides of nitrogen	causes global warming
	sulfur dioxide	photochemical smog
		increased cancer risk

b   Why is carbon monoxide toxic to humans?

    ....

c   Which acids are produced from the gases you have identified as causing acid rain?

    ....

d   Which gas is the second most abundant greenhouse gas in the atmosphere?

    ....

e   Give two specific sources of this gas.

    ....

TIP

Although carbon dioxide is an essential part of clean air (0.04%), it is considered to be a pollutant if the percentage in the air increases.

Challenge

3 Here are a number of methods, labelled from A to F, which could be used to reduce the quantities of pollutants in the atmosphere. In each case, the method is linked to the gas or gases it is designed to help control.

A	Stop using fossil fuels to generate electricity. Use wind and solar power instead.	→	carbon dioxide
B	Stop using gas to heat homes and use electricity instead.	→	carbon dioxide
C	React gases from power stations with calcium oxide (desulfurisation).	→	sulfur dioxide
D	Breed fewer cattle.	→	methane
E	Use electric vehicles instead of those burning fossil fuels.	→	carbon dioxide, carbon monoxide, particulates and oxides of nitrogen
F	Use catalytic converters to clean exhaust gases from cars and other vehicles.	→	carbon monoxide and oxides of nitrogen

a Which two methods would have the greatest effect on global warming? Explain your answer.

....

....

....

b Which two methods would be easiest to implement? Explain your answer.

....

....

....

c Explain why your answers demonstrate the problems of tackling air pollution.

....

....

....

....

4 The fuel for petrol and diesel vehicles does not contain any nitrogenous compounds.

a Explain how the exhaust gases from such vehicles contains harmful oxides of nitrogen (NO_x).

....

....

....

....

b Modern vehicles are fitted with catalytic converters to remove oxides of nitrogen and carbon monoxide. Complete the following symbol equation for one of the reactions that takes place in such a converter.

$$2CO(g) + 2NO(g) \rightarrow \text{.........................} + \text{.........................}$$

c What type of agent is the nitrogen(II) oxide acting as in this equation?

....

> Carbon dioxide, methane and climate change

KEY WORDS

greenhouse effect: the natural phenomenon in which thermal energy from the Sun is 'trapped' at the Earth's surface by certain gases in the atmosphere (greenhouse gases)

greenhouse gas: a gas that absorbs heat reflected from the surface of the Earth, stopping it escaping the atmosphere

Exercise 17.2

IN THIS EXERCISE YOU WILL:

- describe carbon dioxide and methane as greenhouse gases

- investigate how levels of carbon dioxide are linked to increased global warming

- extrapolate data from a graph to make predictions about climate change

- investigate the causes and effects of global warming and strategies to reduce the effects of these environmental issues

> describe how greenhouse gases cause global warming.

Focus

5   Using the words provided, complete the following paragraphs.

   atmosphere   carbon dioxide   gases   global warming   greenhouse

   industrial   life   methane   water   weather

The .... effect has kept the Earth at a temperature suitable for the development

of .... for many thousands of years. As .... activity has

increased during the 20th century, more and more greenhouse gases have been released into

the .... Carbon dioxide and methane are the two .... causing

the greatest problem. .... is 25 times more potent as a greenhouse gas but

.... is present in greater quantities.

Because of these gases, more of the heat from the sun is kept within the Earth's atmosphere

and this causes .... Much of this heat warms .... in the

oceans, which cover about 70% of the Earth's surface. Increased temperatures in the oceans

and in the atmosphere have an effect on the Earth's climate. This effect means that extreme

.... events are more likely.

Practice

6   The data in Table 17.2 show the concentration of carbon dioxide in the atmosphere from 1880 to 2020 and also the mean average temperature of the Earth over the same period.

Year	CO_2 concentration / ppm	Mean average temperature / °C	Year	CO_2 concentration / ppm	Mean average temperature / °C
1880	290	13.9	1992	356	14.1
1900	297	13.9	1996	361	14.3
1920	303	13.8	2000	369	14.4
1940	309	14.1	2004	377	14.6
1960	317	14.0	2008	385	14.5
1980	338	14.3	2012	394	14.6
1984	343	14.1	2016	403	14.7
1988	351	14.4	2020	413	14.9

Table 17.2: Atmospheric carbon dioxide concentration and mean temperature of the Earth from 1880 to 2020.

a Plot two graphs on the grid provided to show the variation of carbon dioxide (left axis) and temperature (right axis) between 1880 and 2020.

> **TIP**
>
> When drawing two graphs on the same axes, use a different symbol for each variable, e.g. a cross (×) for one variable and a dot in a circle (⊙) for the other variable, and identify each variable using a key or label.

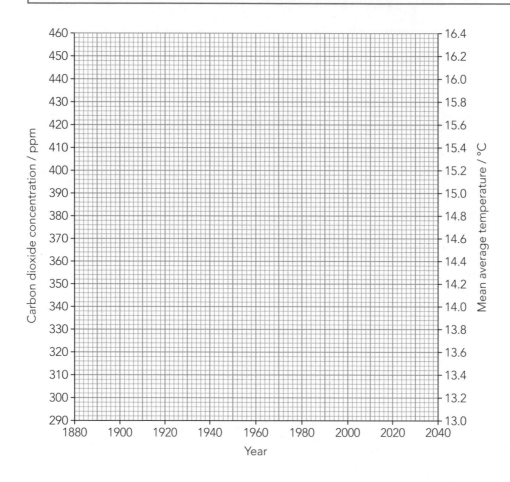

b Describe the trends in carbon dioxide level and mean average temperature from 1880 to 2020.

   i Carbon dioxide:

    ....

    ....

   ii Mean temperature:

    ....

    ....

c   Between 1988 and 1992 the mean average temperature of the Earth decreased. Does this mean that the global atmosphere is not warming? Explain your answer.

....

....

d   Using your graph, predict the likely quantity of carbon dioxide and the likely mean average temperature in 2040.

....

Challenge

7   Figure 17.1 is an incomplete mind map showing the causes and effects of global warming.

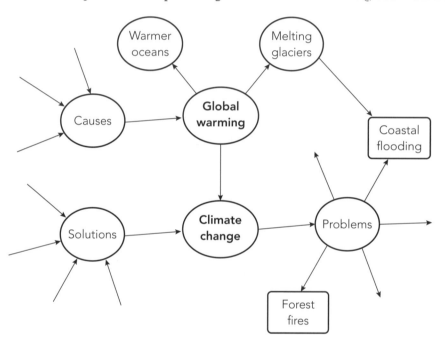

Figure 17.1: Mind map for global warming and climate change.

a   Why would melting glaciers lead to coastal flooding?

....

b   Why might lack of rain cause more forest fires?

....

c   Complete the mind map by adding:

  • more of the problems caused by climate change

  • a number of causes of global warming

  • some ways in which the problems of climate change might be solved.

> **PEER ASSESSMENT**
>
> Compare your mind map with others in your group and try to make a combined version using the best parts of each attempt. What features did all of the completed mind maps have in common? Did you miss any important features from your mind map?

8   Plants can help reduce global warming by taking in carbon dioxide from the air to produce glucose and oxygen.

   a   What is the name of this process?

   ....

   b   Write the word equation for this process.

   ....

   c   Write the balanced symbol equation for this process.

   ....

9   Using the words provided, complete the description of the greenhouse effect in the following paragraphs.

   absorbed   activities   atmosphere   climate   energy

   gases   global   infrared   loss   methane   natural   oceans

   radiated   re-emit   reflected   Sun   temperature   trapping

   The greenhouse effect is a .... phenomenon that warms the surface of the Earth.

   When thermal .... (........................... radiation) from the ....

   reaches the Earth's ...., around 30% is .... back to space and

   around 70% is .... by the oceans and land to heat the planet. Some of this heat is

   then .... back up into the atmosphere.

   Greenhouse .... in the atmosphere such as carbon dioxide and ....

   can absorb this infrared radiation and then .... it back toward the Earth. This

   reduces heat .... to space and keeps the Earth's .... warm enough

   to sustain life.

   Human .... are increasing the amount of greenhouse gases released into the

   atmosphere, ... extra heat and causing .... temperatures to rise.

   This warming of both the atmosphere and the .... gives rise to the different

   aspects of .... change.

> Water

Exercise 17.3

IN THIS EXERCISE YOU WILL:

- describe how water from natural sources contains a variety of substances and investigate how water is purified during water treatment

- describe different ways of testing for the presence and purity of water

- explain why distilled water is used in preference to ordinary tap water in practical chemistry experiments

- develop an understanding of how natural water becomes polluted through human activity.

Focus

10 Drinking water is often obtained from rivers. River water may contain a mixture of the following impurities:

  A   twigs and leaves

  B   plastic bags and bottles

  C   phosphates from detergents from homes and factories

  D   metals and minerals dissolved from rocks and other sources

  E   sewage and animal waste

  F   bacteria and other microbes from sewage

  G   nitrates from fertiliser washed from farm fields (run-off)

  H   sand and soil.

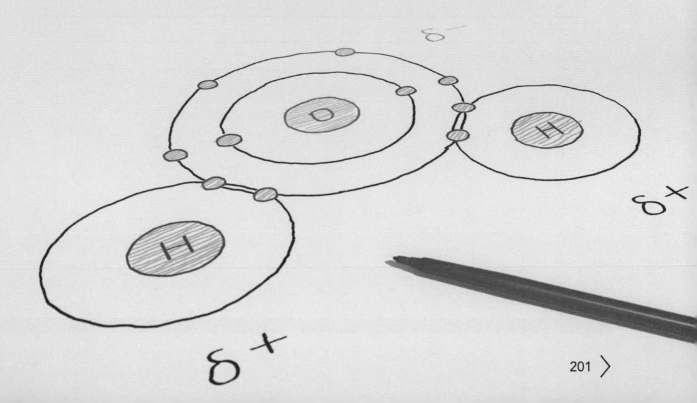

Figure 17.2 shows the stages in the purification of drinking water.

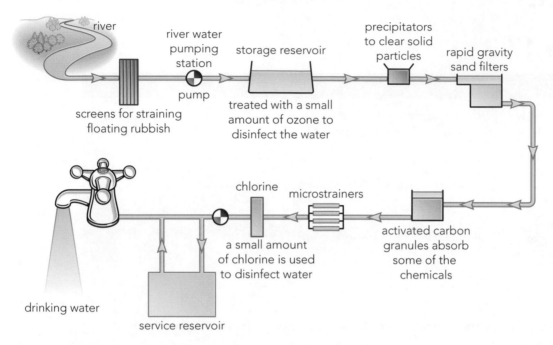

Figure 17.2: Purifying water for the industrial and domestic supply.

Complete Table 17.3 with the letter of each impurity from **A** to **G** to show how water treatment deals with the impurity.

Stage of treatment	What is removed
passed through a coarse screen	
sedimentation and filtration	
chlorination	
not removed in water treatment	

Table 17.3: Stages of water treatment.

Practice

11 A chemist is testing two samples of water: one sample from the sea and one sample from a river.

Use the answers in the list to complete Table 17.4 to show the results that the chemist should get. An answer may be used once, more than once or not at all.

- Boiled at slightly over 100 °C.

- Changed from white to blue.

- Changed from pink to blue.

- There was a lot of white solid remaining.

- Boiled at 103–105 °C.

- There was very little solid remaining.

- Changed from blue to pink.

Test	Seawater	River water
Add to anhydrous copper sulfate		
Test with cobalt chloride paper		
Measure the boiling point		
Boil away a sample of water		

Table 17.4: Results of tests on seawater and river water.

> **TIP**
>
> Seawater contains a large quantity of dissolved salt and other minerals.

12 Explain why distilled water is used in preference to ordinary tap water in practical chemistry experiments.

....

....

....

Challenge

13 Most countries in the world have areas where there is no piped water supply. People in these areas have to rely on water from rivers, streams or wells.

- Water from wells is usually less polluted than water from rivers.

- All untreated water can contain harmful microbes.

- Boiling water kills most harmful microbes.

- Treated water can be supplied in bottles or tanks.

- Chemical tablets can be added to water to kill harmful microbes.

- People use water for many different things (e.g. watering crops, washing, cooking, flushing toilets, drinking).

a   Why is water from wells usually less polluted than water from rivers?

   ....

b   Is pure (treated) water needed for all of the different uses? Explain your answer.

   ....

   ....

c   Well water often contains dissolved minerals. Why can this be a good thing?

   ....

d   Why is it not necessary to use treated water when boiling food during cooking?

   ....

e   Bottled water is often supplied for drinking. Why can this be bad for the environment?

   ....

f   What alternative to bottled water could be used to provide safe drinking water?

   ....

Introduction to organic chemistry

> Molecular structures of organic compounds

KEY WORDS

displayed formula: a representation of the structure of a compound which shows all the atoms and bonds in the molecule

empirical formula: a formula for a compound which shows the simplest ratio of atoms present

functional group: the atom or group of atoms responsible for the characteristic reactions of a compound

homologous series: a family of similar compounds with similar chemical properties due to the presence of the same functional group

hydrocarbons: organic compounds that contain carbon and hydrogen only; the alkanes and alkenes are two series of hydrocarbons

isomers: compounds which have the same molecular formula but different structural arrangements of the atoms – they have different structural formulae

saturated hydrocarbons: hydrocarbon molecules in which all the carbon–carbon bonds are single covalent bonds

structural formula: the structural formula of an organic molecule shows how all the groups of atoms are arranged in the structure; ethanol, CH_3CH_2OH, for example

unsaturated hydrocarbons: hydrocarbons whose molecules contain at least one carbon–carbon double or triple bond

Exercise 18.1

IN THIS EXERCISE YOU WILL:

- investigate the hydrocarbons and identify saturated and unsaturated hydrocarbons
- describe homologous series of compounds as having the same general formula and functional group.

Focus

1   Using the words provided, complete the passage on compounds containing carbon and hydrogen (not all of the words are used).

alkanes   alkenes   bromine   chains   chlorine   colourless   double   ethane

ethene   hydrogen   methane   petroleum   propane

The chief source of organic compounds is the naturally occurring mixture of hydrocarbons

known as .... Hydrocarbons are compounds that contain carbon and

.... only. There are many hydrocarbons because of the ability of carbon atoms to

join together to form long .... There is a series of hydrocarbons with just single

covalent bonds between the carbon atoms in the molecule. These are saturated hydrocarbons,

and they are called .... The simplest of these saturated hydrocarbons has the

formula CH_4 and is called .... Unsaturated hydrocarbons can also occur.

These molecules contain at least one carbon–carbon .... bond.

These compounds belong to the ...., a second series of hydrocarbons.

The simplest of this 'family' of unsaturated hydrocarbons has the formula C_2H_4 and is

known as ....

The test for an unsaturated hydrocarbon is to add the sample to .... water.

It changes colour from orange–brown to .... if the hydrocarbon is unsaturated.

2 Table 18.1 shows the names, formulae and boiling points of the first members of the family of unsaturated hydrocarbons.

a Complete the table.

Name	Formula	Boiling point / °C
	C_2H_4	−102
propene	C_3H_6	−48
butene	C_4H_8	−7
pentene	C_5H_{10}	30
hexene		

Table 18.1: The first members of the alkene series.

b Deduce the molecular formula of the alkene which has a relative molecular mass of 168. (A_r: C = 12, H = 1)

....

c Deduce the general formula of members of the series of compounds shown in Table 18.1 (using n to represent the number of carbon atoms in the molecule).

....

d This family of compounds is an example of a homologous series. What is meant by the term homologous series?

....

....

e What is the functional group that gives this series its characteristic chemical properties?

....

Exercise 18.2

IN THIS EXERCISE YOU WILL:

- investigate and identify different homologous series
- name and draw the displayed formulae of members of the alkanes, alkenes, alcohols and carboxylic acids.

Practice

3 Several different homologous series exist, each with a distinctive functional group in the molecule. Which homologous series do these compounds belong to?

a butane ....   **c** ethanoic acid ....

b propanol ....   **d** heptene ....

4 The name and molecular formula of a compound can be deduced from knowing the homologous series it belongs to and the number of carbon atoms present.

Give the name of the following compounds.

a The alkane with four carbon atoms in the chain: ....

b The carboxylic acid with just one carbon atom: ....

c The alcohol with four carbon atoms: ....

5 The members of a particular homologous series have molecular formulae that fit with a general formula for that series. What is the general formula for the following series (using *n* to represent the number of carbon atoms in the molecule)?

a Alkanes:

....

b Alcohols:

....

c Carboxylic acids:

....

> **TIP**
>
> When looking at the general formula for the carboxylic acids, it is important to realise that the carbon atom of the acid group is counted as part of the chain.

6 The full structure of an organic compound can be represented by its displayed formula. Complete Table 18.2, which lists the molecular and displayed formulae of members of several homologous series.

Name of compound	Homologous series	Molecular formula	Displayed formula
propanol			
ethanoic acid		CH_3COOH	
propene		C_3H_6	
ethanol	an alcohol		
ethane	an alkane	C_2H_6	

Table 18.2: The displayed formulae of several different organic compounds.

SELF-ASSESSMENT

Look at your answers to question **6** and use the following definitions to help check your answers.

- Alcohols: a series of organic compounds containing the functional group –OH and with the general formula $C_nH_{2n+1}OH$

- Alkanes: a series of hydrocarbons with the general formula C_nH_{2n+2}; they are saturated compounds, as they have only single bonds between carbon atoms in their structure

- Alkenes: a series of hydrocarbons with the general formula C_nH_{2n}; they are unsaturated molecules, as they have a C=C double bond somewhere in the chain

- Carboxylic acids: a family of organic compounds containing the functional group –COOH (–CO_2H), with the general formula $C_nH_{2n+1}COOH$

With a partner, discuss the difference between a molecular formula and a displayed formula. What clear, additional information is given by the displayed formula that is not obvious in the molecular formula? Is this clear in the displayed formulae you have drawn?

Exercise 18.3

IN THIS EXERCISE YOU WILL:

- name and draw different types of formulae of members of various homologous series

- show how structural formulae can be used to represent molecules.

Challenge

7   A molecule of an organic compound can be represented by two other types of formulae which give useful information on the composition of the compound.

The structural formula of the molecule can be represented without drawing its full displayed formula. The empirical formula shows the simplest whole number ratio of the elements present.

Complete Table 18.3, in which the structural and empirical formulae of some typical compounds are listed.

Compound	Molecular formula	Structural formula	Empirical formula
butane	C_4H_{10}		C_2H_5
propene	C_3H_6	$CH_3CH=CH_2$	
ethanol	C_2H_5OH		
propanoic acid	C_2H_5COOH		
propyl ethanoate	$CH_3COOC_2H_5$		

Table 18.3: The empirical and structural formulae of some organic compounds.

8   Figure 18.1 lists some complex organic molecules showing the range of organic structures, involving rings of carbon atoms as well as chains. Use information from the structures to answer the following questions.

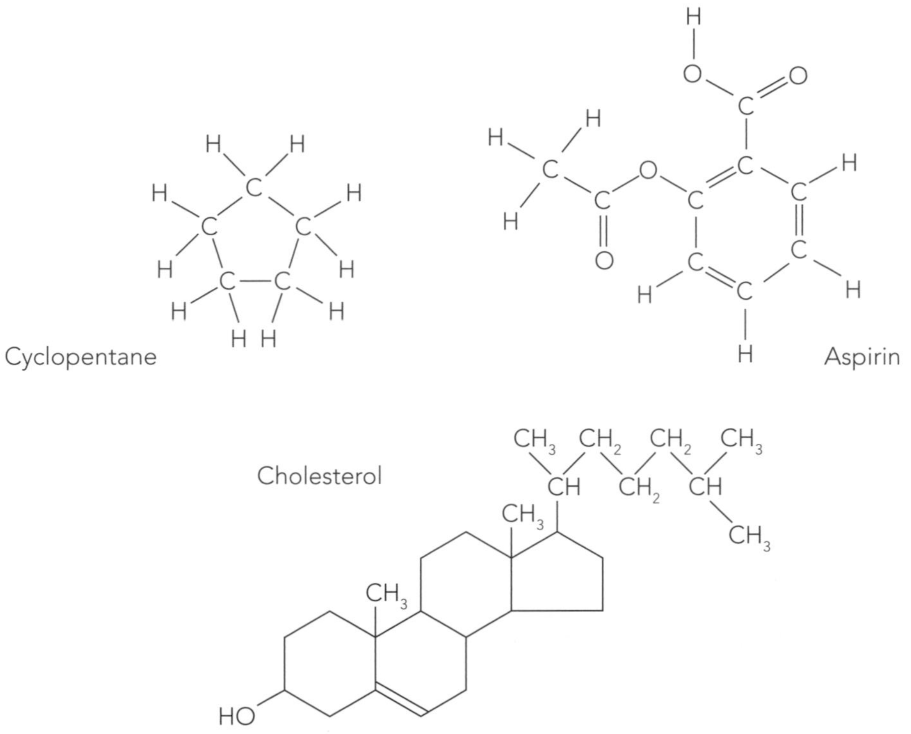

Figure 18.1: Some organic structures involving chains and rings of carbon atoms (note that cyclopentane and aspirin are shown as displayed formulae; while cholesterol is given as a structural formula so as not to be too distracting).

a   Why does the name cyclopentane have the ending -*ane*?

....

b   Circle the carboxylic acid group in the structure of aspirin (label the group 'A').

c   Aspirin also contains a link characteristic of an ester. Circle the ester link in the molecule (label the link 'B').

....

d   Which group present in the structure of cholesterol gives rise to the name ending (-ol) of this compound?

....

> **TIP**
>
> It is important to be able to relate your knowledge and understanding to situations that you have not dealt with directly. The key is to be clear in your understanding of the ideas you have covered and not be distracted by the surrounding additional information presented by the context.

9 Cyclopentane has the molecular formula C_5H_{10} (Figure 18.1).

    a What is the structural formula of another hydrocarbon that also has this molecular formula? Which homologous series does it belong to?

    ....

    b What is the name given to this phenomenon where two (or more) molecules can have the same molecular formula but different structures?

    ....

10 For each of the following examples, give the name and structural formula of another molecule with the same molecular formula but a different structure.

    a 2-methylpropane, $CH_3CH(CH_3)CH_3$

    ....

    b butan-1-ol, $CH_3CH_2CH_2CH_2OH$

    ....

    c but-2-ene, $CH_3CH=CHCH_3$

    ....

    d 1,2-dibromoethane, CH_2BrCH_2Br

    ....

    e methyl propanoate, $CH_3CH_2COOCH_3$

    ....

11 Which ester would be formed using the following unbranched alcohols and carboxylic acids? Give the name and structural formula.

    a propanol and propanoic acid

    ....

    Draw the displayed formula of this ester.

    b methanol and butanoic acid

    ....

    Draw the displayed formula of this ester.

Chapter 19

Reactions of organic compounds

> Characteristic reactions of alkanes and alkenes

KEY WORDS

addition reaction: a reaction in which a simple molecule adds across the carbon–carbon double bond of an alkene

photochemical reaction: a chemical reaction where the activation energy required to start the reaction is provided by light, usually of a particular wavelength, falling on the reactants

structural isomerism: a property of compounds that have the same molecular formula but different structural formulae; the individual compounds are known as structural isomers

substitution reaction: a reaction in which an atom (or atoms) of a molecule is (are) replaced by different atom(s), without changing the molecule's general structure

Exercise 19.1

IN THIS EXERCISE YOU WILL:

- use knowledge of empirical and molecular formulae

- investigate the characteristic reactions of members of different homologous series

- distinguish between saturated and unsaturated hydrocarbons by observing the presence or absence of double bonds in their displayed formulae

- describe how unsaturated hydrocarbons are much more reactive than saturated hydrocarbons as they can take part in addition reactions

- consider the substitution reactions of alkanes with halogens in the presence of ultraviolet light.

Focus

1   **a**   Complete Table 19.1 on the two hydrocarbons both having a structure involving two carbon atoms. (A_r: H = 1, C = 12)

Name of hydrocarbon	ethane	ethene
Molecular formula of hydrocarbon	C_2H_6	
Saturated / unsaturated		
Displayed formula of hydrocarbon		
Relative molecular mass of hydrocarbon		

Table 19.1: The formulae of two hydrocarbons.

   b   Explain both your answers to the question on saturated/unsaturated in Table 19.1.

     i   Ethane:

     ....

     ii   Ethene:

     ....

   c   Ethene belongs to a homologous series. Name this homologous series and give the functional group present.

   ....

Practice

2   Limonene is a colourless unsaturated hydrocarbon found in oranges and lemons. The structure of limonene is shown in Figure 19.1.

   a   On the structure shown, draw a circle around the bonds which make limonene an unsaturated hydrocarbon.

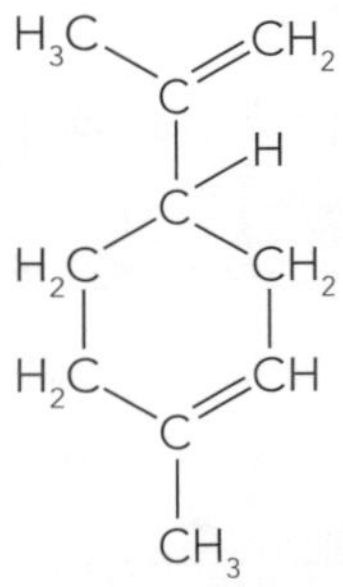

Figure 19.1: Structure of limonene.

b What is the molecular formula of limonene?

....

c Calculate the relative molecular mass of limonene.

....

d Describe the colour change which occurs when excess limonene is added to a few drops of bromine water.

....

e Figure 19.2 shows how limonene can be extracted from lemon peel by steam distillation.

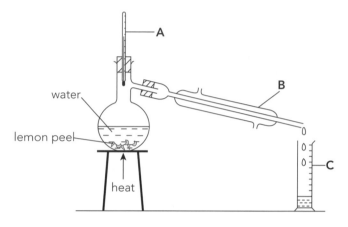

Figure 19.2: Extraction of limonene by steam distillation.

Name the pieces of apparatus labelled A, B and C.

A ....

B ....

C ....

f When limonene undergoes incomplete combustion, carbon monoxide is formed. What do you understand by the term incomplete combustion?

....

....

> **TIP**
>
> You should develop the ability to apply knowledge gained from studying the major examples of a particular type of compound to unusual examples of such compounds that you may not have seen before. Do not be distracted by the unusual details but focus on the features that are common to both examples.

Challenge

3   There are three compounds with the formula C_4H_8. The partial displayed formulae of two of them are shown in Figure 19.3.

   a   Complete the two displayed formulae by adding the hydrogen atoms.

   C=C–C–C   C–C=C–C

   Figure 19.3: Displayed formulae of two compounds with the formula C_4H_8.

   b   In the space below, draw the displayed formulae of the compounds formed when the compounds shown in Figure 19.3 react with bromine.

   c   Using the molecular formula, write the balanced symbol equation for the reaction of both isomers with bromine.

   ....

4   Chlorine reacts with alkanes in a substitution reaction. Hydrogen chloride is the inorganic product:

   propane + chlorine → chloropropane + hydrogen chloride

   a   Draw the displayed formula of propane.

   b   Draw the displayed formulae of the two isomers of chloropropane.

c   The reaction between propane and chlorine is a photochemical reaction. Suggest what is meant by the term photochemical reaction.

....

....

....

> **TIP**
>
> Both substitution and addition reactions usually involve two reactants, but in a substitution reaction two products are formed whereas in an addition reaction just one product is formed.

> The production of alcohols

KEY WORDS

catalytic cracking: the decomposition of long-chain alkanes into alkenes and alkanes of lower relative molecular mass; involves passing the larger alkane molecules over a catalyst heated to 500 °C

fermentation: a reaction carried out using a living organism, usually a yeast or bacteria, to produce a useful chemical compound; most usually refers to the production of ethanol

Exercise 19.2

IN THIS EXERCISE YOU WILL:

- draw the displayed formulae of some short chain alcohols

- calculate the molecular formula of an alcohol from its displayed formula and from this calculate its relative molecular mass

- investigate the industrial preparation of ethanol by different methods

- describe how catalytic cracking produces useful alkenes that can be used to make other important compounds

> investigate the reactions of alcohols.

Focus

5 **a** In the space provided, draw the displayed formula for the alcohol, ethanol.

b The general formula for the alcohols is $C_nH_{2n+1}OH$. Give the formula for the alcohol with three carbons.

....

c Calculate its relative molecular mass. (A_r: C = 12, H = 1, O = 16)

....

6 **a** The names of some naturally occurring compounds are listed. Circle those names that are alcohols.

cholesterol   geraniol   limonene   retinal   retinol   squalene

b To which homologous series do squalene and limonene belong?

....

Practice

7 The equation for the formation of ethanol from ethene can be written as follows.

$$C_2H_4(g) + H_2O(g) \rightleftharpoons C_2H_5OH(g)$$

a Explain why the reaction is carried out at temperatures above 100 °C.

....

b Explain why the reaction is carried out at high pressure.

....

....

8   The fermentation (anaerobic respiration) of glucose by yeast can be represented by the following equation. The reaction is catalysed by the enzymes found in yeast. After a few days, the reaction stops. It has produced a 12% aqueous solution of ethanol.

$$C_6H_{12}O_6 \rightarrow 2C_2H_5OH + 2CO_2$$

a   Sketch a labelled diagram to show how fermentation can be carried out.

b   Suggest a reason why the reaction stops after a few days.

....

....

c   Why is it essential that there is no oxygen in the reaction vessel?

....

....

d   Give one advantage each for the production of ethanol from ethene and sugar (glucose). Your answer should refer to the methods of production and not whether the sources are renewable or non-renewable.

Advantage using ethene:

....

....

Advantage using sugar:

....

....

SELF-ASSESSMENT

Drawing diagrams to represent experimental apparatus and chemical structures is an important skill. Clarity of drawing and labelling are important aspects. In the diagram you have drawn in this question, are you confident that you have included all the relevant information? Can your diagram be easily understood by others?

Challenge

9 Butan-1-ol is an increasingly important alcohol which can be made in the laboratory and in industry in a variety of different ways. Industrially, it can then be used as a solvent for paints and varnishes, to make esters, and as a fuel.

Industrially, butan-1-ol can be manufactured from but-1-ene, which is made from petroleum. But-1-ene can be obtained from alkanes such as nonane, C_9H_{20}, by catalytic cracking.

a Give the reaction conditions required for cracking.

....

b Complete the equation for the cracking of nonane, C_9H_{20}, to give but-1-ene as one of the products.

$C_9H_{20} \rightarrow$ ....

c Name the reagent that reacts with but-1-ene to form butan-1-ol.

....

10 Butan-1-ol takes part in the characteristic reactions of alcohols.

a Balance the equation for the complete combustion of butan-1-ol.

$C_4H_9OH +$ ....$O_2 \rightarrow$ ....$CO_2 +$ ....H_2O

b Write a word equation for the preparation of the ester butyl propanoate.

....

c What is the structural formula of butyl propanoate?

....

> **TIP**
>
> The first part of the name of an ester tells you the identity of the original alcohol, while the second part indicates the acid involved in forming the ester.

> Alcohols as fuels

KEY WORD
fuel: a substance that can be used as a source of energy, usually by burning (combustion)

Exercise 19.3

IN THIS EXERCISE YOU WILL:

- show why ethanol, and other alcohols, are useful fuels
- name and give the structural formula of an isomer.

Focus

11 Ethanol is a good fuel. It burns with a clear flame and gives out lots of heat. It is also a liquid at room temperature and therefore easily transported.

    a Give the equation for the complete combustion of ethanol.

    ....

    b Give the equation for the products of the incomplete combustion of ethanol.

    ....

    c Give five reasons why ethanol is a good fuel.

    ....

    ....

    ....

    ....

    ....

    d Ethanol made from ethene is a non-renewable fuel, but ethanol made from glucose is a renewable fuel. Using ethanol as an example, explain 'non-renewable' and 'renewable'.

    ....

    ....

    ....

Practice

12 A student used the apparatus shown in Figure 19.4 to investigate the amount of heat produced when ethanol was burnt.

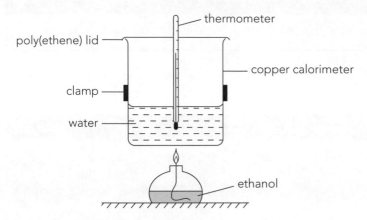

Figure 19.4: Experiment with ethanol as a fuel.

a What measurements are made during this investigation?

....

....

b If the heat change for the reaction was measured, it would be less exothermic than it should be. Give two errors that mean that the measurements made are inaccurate.

....

....

c Complete the equation for the complete combustion of ethanol.

$C_2H_5OH + 3O_2 \rightarrow$ .... $CO_2 +$ .... H_2O

d When 2.3 g of ethanol is burnt, 2.7 g of water is formed. Calculate the mass of water formed when 13.8 g of ethanol is burnt.

....

Challenge

13 Alcohols are a homologous series which have similar chemical properties and a gradual change in physical properties. The use of an alcohol as a fuel depends on the amount of alcohol vapour present, which is dependent on the boiling point of the alcohol. The boiling points of some straight-chain alcohols are shown in Table 19.2.

Name of alcohol	Structure	Relative molecular mass of alcohol (C = 12, H = 1, O = 16)	Boiling point / °C
methanol	CH_3OH	32	65
A:	CH_3CH_2OH	46	78
propan-1-ol	$CH_3CH_2CH_2OH$	60	D:
butan-1-ol	$CH_3CH_2CH_2CH_2OH$	74	118
pentan-1-ol	B:	C:	138

Table 19.2: Some straight-chain alcohols.

a Complete the table by filling in the gaps for A–C.

b Imagine that you are given some graph paper and the data in Table 19.2. Explain how you would use the data to estimate the boiling point of an alcohol using a graph. Your explanation should include the following:

- what you would plot as the independent variable and what you would use as the dependent variable

- how you would plot the graph

- how you would use the graph to estimate the boiling points of propan-1-ol (use this to complete the gap for D in Table 19.2) and hexan-1-ol.

....

....

....

....

....

....

c Explain which of your estimates you are least confident about, propan-1-ol or hexan-1-ol.

....

....

....

> The preparation and reactions of carboxylic acids

KEY WORDS

carboxylic acids: a homologous series of organic compounds containing the functional group –COOH (–CO$_2$H), with the general formula C$_n$H$_{2n+1}$COOH

esters: a family of organic compounds formed by esterification, characterised by strong and pleasant tastes and smells

Exercise 19.4

IN THIS EXERCISE YOU WILL:

- distinguish between the displayed formulae for alcohols and carboxylic acids

- consider the reactions of ethanoic acid as a weak acid

> investigate how ethanol is oxidised to ethanoic acid and how alcohols react with carboxylic acids to produce esters

> understand that esters are formed by reactions between alcohols and carboxylic acids.

Focus

14 Figure 19.5 shows some alcohols, carboxylic acids and esters.

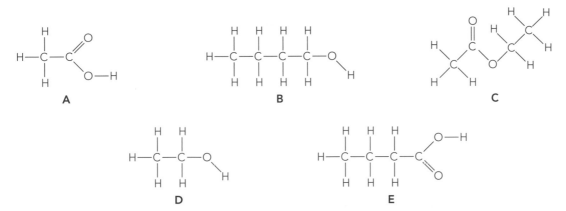

Figure 19.5: Structural formulae of some alcohols, carboxylic acids and esters.

Answer the following questions about compounds A–E.

a Give the letter for the compound ethanoic acid. ....

b Give the letters for the two compounds that have the molecular formula $C_4H_8O_2$.

....

c Give the letter for the compound formed by fermentation of sugar. ....

d Give the letters for the two compounds that are alcohols. ....

e Give the letter for the compound that has the molecular formula $C_2H_4O_2$.

....

f What is the empirical formula of compound C? ....

Practice

15 a Ethanoic acid is formed by the oxidation of ethanol. The unfinished equation for the reaction is shown below. (The symbol [O] represents oxygen from the oxidising agent.)

$$CH_3CH_2OH + 2[O] \rightarrow CH_3COOH + ...$$

Identify the missing product.

b What mass of ethanoic acid can be formed from 920 kg of ethanol?

....

....

....

....

TIP

Always show your working clearly in any calculations so that you can check your work.

c   Ethanoic acid reacts with sodium carbonate. Write the word equation for this reaction.

....

Challenge

16 Acidified potassium manganate(VII) was used to oxidise ethanol to ethanoic acid using the apparatus shown in Figure 19.6.

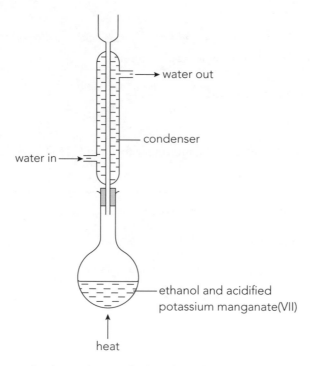

Figure 19.6: Apparatus for the oxidation of ethanol to ethanoic acid.

a   Comment on what might happen if the upright condenser were changed to the usual slightly sloping arrangement. (Note that the boiling points of ethanol and ethanoic acid are 78°C and 118°C, respectively.)

....

....

b   Complete the following symbol equation for the oxidation of ethanol to ethanoic acid:

C_2H_5OH + ...[O] → CH_3COOH + ...

c A group of students were asked to prepare the ester ethyl ethanoate with ethanol as the only organic reagent available. The procedure they were given is described in the paragraph. Complete the paragraph.

The group knew that they needed .... acid as well as ethanol to prepare

ethyl ethanoate. So, they took the ethanol and divided it into two portions. One

portion was oxidised to .... acid by adding it to ....

potassium .... (VII). The mixture was then refluxed for an hour and the

.... acid produced was distilled off. The ethanoic acid was then mixed

with the .... and some concentrated .... acid added. The

concentrated .... acid acted as a .... for the reaction. After

the mixture was refluxed together, the ester .... ethanoate was distilled off.

d Complete the following equation for the preparation of the ester.

$$CH_3COOH(l) + C_2H_5OH(l) \rightleftharpoons CH_3COOC_2H_5(l) + \text{.........................} (l)$$

> Chapter 20

Petrochemicals and polymers

> Refining petroleum

KEY WORDS

fractional distillation: a method of distillation using a fractionating column used to separate liquids with different boiling points

petroleum (or crude oil): a fossil fuel formed underground over many millions of years by conditions of high pressure and temperature acting on the remains of dead sea creatures

Exercise 20.1

IN THIS EXERCISE YOU WILL:

- discuss the fractions obtained from the distillation of petroleum and their major uses

- plot a bar chart and interpret data from the chart

- show how catalytic cracking can be used to produce shorter alkanes and alkenes from the larger alkanes of the lower fractions.

Focus

Petroleum (crude oil) is a raw material which is processed in an oil refinery. Two of the processes used are fractional distillation and catalytic cracking.

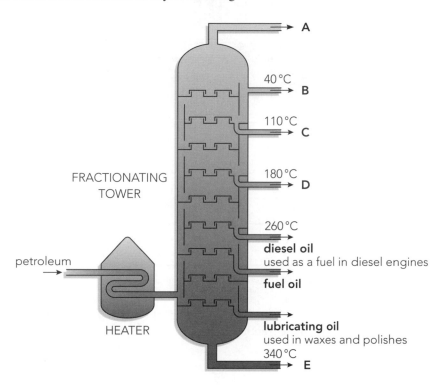

Figure 20.1: The fractional distillation of petroleum.

1   Figure 20.1 shows the fractional distillation of petroleum. Give the name and a major use for each fraction.

A   ....

B   ....

C   ....

D   ....

E   ....

2   a   Which physical property is used to separate petroleum by fractional distillation?

   ....

   b   How do the chain length of the molecules present and the viscosity of the fractions vary as you ascend the fractionating tower?

   ....

   ....

Practice

3 Table 20.1 gives information on the proportions of certain fractions in a sample of petroleum from a particular oil-producing region. It also shows the commercial demand for these fractions.

Fraction	Number of carbon atoms per molecule	Proportion in petroleum / %	Percentage needed by the oil refinery to supply demand / %
A	1–4	2	5
B	4–12	8	22
C	7–14	10	5
D	12–16	16	11
diesel oil	14–18	19	23
fuel oil, waxes and E	over 20	45	34

Table 20.1: Supply and demand for the different fractions from the distillation of petroleum.

a Plot a bar chart of the two sets of figures for each of the fractions mentioned in Table 20.1 to compare the availability and demand for these fractions.

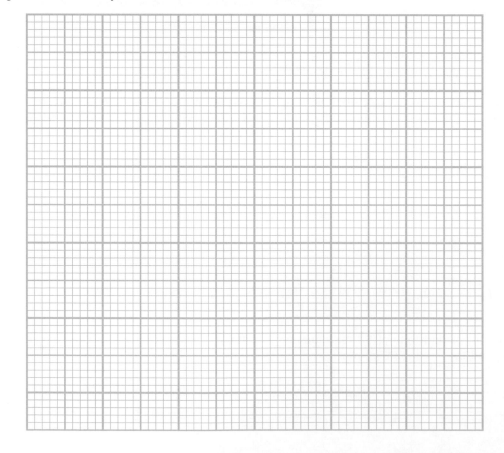

The differences between these two sets of figures highlight the need for manipulation of the chemistry of the fractions.

b Which fractions are in greatest demand generally?

....

c What is the total proportion of the demand that is used for fuelling cars and lorries (trucks)?

....

SELF-ASSESSMENT

Representing data in a bar chart is not as common in chemistry as drawing a line graph but it is an important skill. Use the checklist below to self-assess the bar chart you drew in question **3**.

For each point, award yourself:

2 marks if you did it really well

1 mark if you made a good attempt at it, and partly succeeded

0 marks if you did not try to do it, or did not succeed.

Checklist	Marks awarded
Have you drawn the axes with a ruler, using most of the width and height of the grid?	
Have you made clear which bars show the proportion in petroleum and which show the percentage in demand?	
Have you labelled all the axes correctly?	
Have you used an appropriate scale for each of your axis?	
Have you drawn your bars clearly and plotted the data correctly?	
Total (out of 10):	

Take a look at where you scored yourself 2 marks and where you gave yourself less than that. What did you do well, and what aspects will you focus on next time?

Challenge

4 The hydrocarbon $C_{15}H_{32}$ can be cracked to make propene and one other hydrocarbon.

   a Write an equation for this reaction.

   ....

   b Draw the displayed formula of propene.

5 Figure 20.2 shows part of the apparatus for cracking decane in the lab.

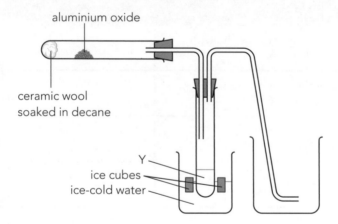

Figure 20.2: An experiment on cracking in the laboratory.

When decane is cracked in the laboratory, liquid octane is formed.

   a Complete this equation for the cracking of decane, and name the gas that is formed:

$$C_{10}H_{22}(l) \rightarrow C_8H_{18}(l) + \text{.........................}$$

         decane   octane   ....

   b Complete the diagram to show how the gas is collected above water.

   c What is the aluminium oxide present in the tube for?

   ....

   d Mark an arrow on Figure 20.2 to show where the test-tube should be heated.

e Identify the liquid marked Y and give the balanced symbol equation for its complete combustion.

....

f Give the test used to identify the gas formed and the result of the test.

Test: ....

Results of test: ....

g Explain why nonane (C_9H_{20}) cannot be a product of the cracking of decane.

....

....

TIP

Be aware of the methods for collecting gases in experiments. In particular, be clear on the different safety methods for avoiding cold water being drawn back into very hot apparatus ('suck back') when collecting a gas over water (including the use of a Bunsen valve).

> Addition polymerisation

KEY WORDS

addition polymer: a polymer formed by an addition reaction – the monomer molecules contain a C=C double bond

monomer: a small molecule, such as ethene, which can be polymerised to make a polymer

polymer: a substance consisting of very large molecules made by polymerising a large number of repeating units, or monomers

polymerisation: the chemical reaction in which molecules (monomers) join together to form a long-chain polymer

Exercise 20.2

IN THIS EXERCISE YOU WILL:

- investigate polymerisation using the synthesis of poly(ethene) as an example of addition polymerisation

- describe the usefulness of plastics and some of the environmental problems they cause

> deduce the repeat unit of an addition polymer.

Focus

6 Poly(ethene) is a major polymer used for making a range of plastic for a wide variety of containers.

    a Using the words provided, complete the sentences about poly(ethene). Not all of the words are used.

acids   **addition**   **condensation**   **ethane**   **ethene**

monomers   **polymer**   **polymerisation**

Poly(ethene) is an .... polymer formed from many ....

molecules. In this reaction, the starting molecules can be described as ....

The process is known as ....

    b Draw the structure of poly(ethene) showing at least three repeat units.

Practice

7 Plastics made from polymers have proved very useful in a wide range of situations. Link the property of a plastic (**a–e**) to their best use (**i–v**) by drawing a line between them.

a plastics do not conduct electricity		**i** plastics can be used to make ropes
b plastics can be strong and have low density		**ii** plastics can be used to make crates and boxes
c plastics can form thin, flexible sheets		**iii** plastics can be used to make food containers
d plastics can make strong fibres		**iv** plastics can be used to make bags
e plastics are not attacked by acids		**v** plastics can be used as insulators

Challenge

8   Figure 20.3 shows the structure of a different addition polymer, X.

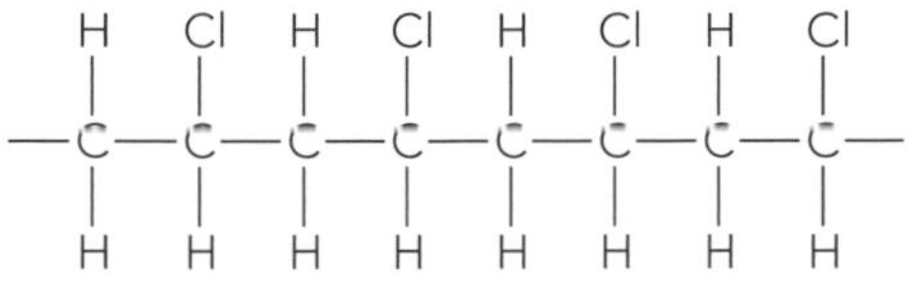

Figure 20.3: The structure of polymer X.

Draw the structure of the monomer from which polymer X is formed.

TIP

Remember when drawing a representation of the structure of a polymer (whether an addition or condensation type), you should always show the continuation bonds at both ends (Figure 20.3).

---

9   a   Poly(ethene) and polymer X are non-biodegradable. Explain what the term non-biodegradable means.

....

....

b   Polymer X can be disposed of by burning at high temperature. However, this can produce toxic waste gases such as hydrogen chloride. Hydrogen chloride can be removed from the waste gases by reaction with moist calcium carbonate powder. Name the three products of this reaction.

....

10   The nature of plastic material and our casual disposal of it means that it forms a major part of the debris that pollutes rivers and oceans.

a   What are the dangers of large pieces of plastic debris for aquatic life?

....

....

....

....

b Plastic microbeads made of polymers such as poly(ethene) find their way into the oceans in very large numbers. What types of product have microbeads that result in this pollution?

....

....

> Synthetic and natural condensation polymers

KEY WORDS

amino acids: naturally occurring organic compounds that possess both an amino (−NH$_2$) group and an acid (−COOH) group in the molecule; there are 20 naturally occurring amino acids and they are polymerised in cells to make proteins

condensation polymer: a polymer formed by a condensation reaction, e.g. nylon is produced by the condensation reaction between 1,6-diaminohexane and hexanedioic acid; this is the type of polymerisation used in biological systems to produce proteins, nucleic acids and polysaccharides

polyamide: a polymer where the repeating units are joined together by amide (peptide) links, e.g. nylon and proteins

polyester: a polymer where the monomer units are joined together by ester links, e.g. PET

proteins: polymers of amino acids formed by a condensation reaction; they have a wide variety of biological functions

Exercise 20.3

IN THIS EXERCISE YOU WILL:

> compare the key features of addition and condensation polymerisation

> identify the simple molecules formed during condensation polymers

> compare addition and condensation polymers

> investigate condensation polymerisation and the formation of polyamides and polyesters

> describe the structures of the synthetic condensation polymers nylon and PET

> describe proteins as natural polyamides formed from amino acids.

Focus

11   Addition polymerisation is a method of making polymers from unsaturated monomers. Other synthetic polymers, such as nylon and PET, are made by a different type of polymerisation involving condensation rather than addition reactions. Table 20.2 lists the main differences between these two types of polymerisation.

Using the words provided, complete the comparisons in Table 20.2.

addition   condensation   double   functional   hydrolysed   one

polymer   two   unsaturated   water

	Addition polymerisation	Condensation polymerisation
Monomers used	usually many molecules of a single .... monomer, usually contains a carbon–carbon .... bond	molecules of .... different monomers usually used; monomers contain a reactive .... group at each end of the molecule
Reaction taking place	an .... reaction	a .... reaction with loss of a small molecule (usually ....) each time a monomer joins the chain
Nature of product	only .... product formed – the polymer	two products: the .... plus another, small, molecule
	non-biodegradable	can be biodegradable
	resistant to acids	PET can be .... back to monomers by acids or alkalis

Table 20.2: Comparing addition and condensation polymerisation.

Practice

12 Condensation polymerisation is important in the formation of both natural and synthetic polymers. The monomers involved are bifunctional. They have functional groups at both ends of the molecule.

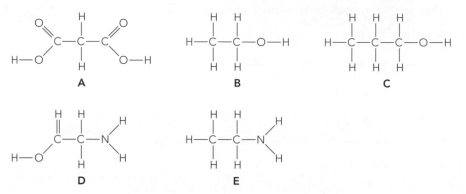

Figure 20.4: Possible condensation polymerisation monomers.

a Which three molecules from those labelled A–E in Figure 20.4 can be used to make a condensation polymer?

....

b Explain why the other two molecules in Figure 20.4 are unable to form a condensation polymer.

....

....

13 There are various types of important condensation polymers. In each case, the reaction to form the polymer can be represented by a schematic diagram which shows only the key interactions between the functional groups and the nature of the linkage involved.

$$H_2N-\boxed{}-NH_2 \quad HOOC-\boxed{}-COOH$$

Figure 20.5: Possible monomers for a condensation polymer.

a What type of polymer can be formed from the monomers represented in Figure 20.5?

Choose from: polyamide, polyester or polysaccharide.

....

b Draw the structure of the polymer formed (show at least three monomers joined together).

c What molecule is eliminated at the formation of each linkage?

....

d What is the name of the most important synthetic polymer of this type?

....

Challenge

14 Complete Table 20.3 on a second type of important condensation polymer.

Monomers used	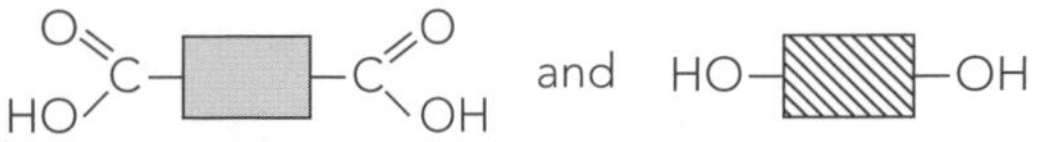
Structure of the polymer formed (show just three monomers joined)	
Other product formed	Name: .... Formula: ....
Type of polymer formed (circle one of these possible answers)	polyamide polyester polysaccharide

Table 20.3: A second important condensation polymer.

> **TIP**
>
> The key features when drawing schematic representations of both natural and synthetic condensation polymers are the functional groups of the monomers involved and the displayed structure of the links in the polymer. When drawing the links in a synthetic polyamide or polyester where each monomer has only one type of functional group, the links in the polymer will alternate in direction.

15 Compare the structure of a protein with that of a synthetic polyamide. The structure of a typical protein is given in Figure 20.6.

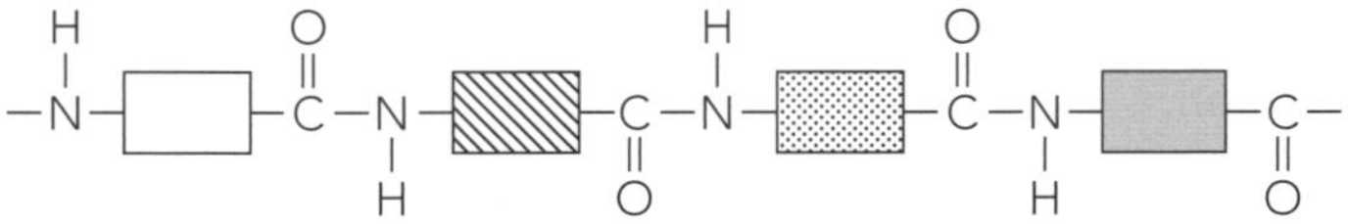

Figure 20.6: The structure of a protein chain.

a How are they similar?

....

b How are they different?

....

....

c What type of monomers are used in synthesising proteins by biological cells?

....

> Chapter 21

Experimental design and separation techniques

> Carrying out a rate experiment

KEY WORDS

volumetric pipette: a pipette used to measure out a volume of solution accurately
---

Exercise 21.1

IN THIS EXERCISE YOU WILL:

- investigate the effect of concentration on rate of reaction

- identify appropriate apparatus for measuring variables

- draw a graph from data and analyse the results

- design an experiment to determine the effect of temperature on rate of reaction.

Focus

When sodium thiosulfate reacts with hydrochloric acid, the following reaction takes place:

$$Na_2S_2O_3(aq) + 2HCl(aq) \rightarrow 2NaCl(aq) + H_2O(aq) + SO_2(g) + S(s)$$

At low temperatures the sulfur dioxide remains dissolved in the water, but sulfur is a solid and it forms a pale yellow precipitate in the solution.

If the flask containing the reaction is placed above a cross (X) drawn on a piece of paper, the precipitate of sulfur particles eventually turns the liquid cloudy and hides the cross (Figure 21.1).

The length of time taken for the cross to 'disappear' can be used to measure the reaction rate.

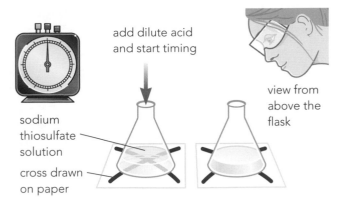

Figure 21.1: The 'disappearing cross' experiment.

A student followed the instructions below to perform an experiment:

- Measure 30 cm³ of sodium thiosulfate and add to the flask on the paper.

- Rapidly add 10 cm³ of hydrochloric acid and immediately start the timer.

- Stop the timer when the cross on the paper can no longer be seen.

- Record the time taken.

- Empty and rinse the flask.

- Repeat the experiment using 25 cm³ of sodium thiosulfate and 5 cm³ of water.

- Repeat four more times. Reduce the volume of sodium thiosulfate by 5 cm³ each time. Increase the volume of water by 5 cm³ each time.

The experimental results are shown in Table 21.1.

Expt No.	Volume of acid / cm³	Volume of sodium thiosulfate / cm³	Volume of water / cm³	Time for cross to disappear / s
1	10	30	0	35
2	10	25	5	42
3	10	20	10	50
4	10	15	15	60
5	10	10	20	100
6	10	5	25	250

Table 21.1: Practical results from the rate experiment.

1   Which piece of apparatus, a measuring cylinder or a volumetric pipette, would be best for adding the acid to the mixture? Give a reason for your answer.

....

....

....

2   A stop clock is used to time this reaction. What advantage, if any, would there be in using a digital timer?

....

Practice

3   Use the results in Table 21.1 to plot a graph of the time taken for the cross to disappear against volume of sodium thiosulfate solution used.

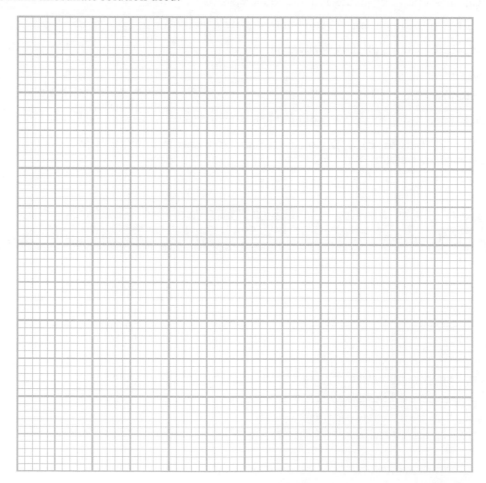

4   **a**   What volume of sodium thiosulfate would have produced a time of 70 seconds?

....

b   What volume of water would have to be added if the experiment were carried out?

....

> **TIP**
>
> Interpreting the shape of the graphs from rate experiments is important. Think about what the shape of the graph tells you about the relationship between rate of reaction and reactant concentration.

5   The original concentration of sodium thiosulfate used in these experiments was $0.5 \, \text{mol/dm}^3$. What was the actual concentration in experiment 3?

....

Challenge

6   This reaction between sodium thiosulfate and hydrochloric acid can also be used to find the effect of temperature on rate of reaction.

a   Describe how you would carry out this reaction. Your description should include any additional apparatus needed and explain how the investigation would be made a fair test by controlling all the variables other than temperature and rate of reaction.

....

....

....

....

....

....

....

....

....

b   Sulfur dioxide is a toxic gas. Why is it necessary to not heat the reaction mixture to a temperature in excess of $50\,°C$?

....

....

SELF-ASSESSMENT

Look at your description of how you would carry out an investigation into the reaction between sodium thiosulfate and hydrochloric acid. Use this checklist to self-assess your description. Have you included:

- additional apparatus needed

- safety considerations

- what measurements you would take and when you would take them

- detail of any repeat measurements you would take

- an explanation of how you would make sure that the experiment was a clear study of how reaction rate varies with temperature (a fair test)?

> Separation and purification

KEY WORDS

distillation: the process of boiling a liquid and then condensing the vapour produced back into a liquid: used to purify liquids and to separate liquids from solutions

filtration: the separation of a solid from a liquid, using a fine filter paper which does not allow the solid to pass through

solvent: the liquid that dissolves the solid solute to form a solution; water is the most common solvent but liquids in organic chemistry that can act as solvents are called organic solvents

Exercise 21.2

IN THIS EXERCISE YOU WILL:

- discuss the differences between elements, mixtures and compounds

- consider a variety of methods used to separate different mixtures

- show how melting point and boiling point can be used to assess the purity of a substance

- design an experiment to determine the composition of an alloy.

Focus

7 a Place each of the following substances into the correct columns in the table.

aluminium   brass   carbon dioxide   copper sulfate   dilute nitric acid

methane   seawater   sodium   zinc

Elements	Mixtures	Compounds

b Which one of these types of substance cannot be separated into different substances? Explain your answer.

....

....

....

c How can pure water be separated into two different substances?

....

Practice

8 Mixtures can be separated into their different components in a number of different ways, some of which are:

- crystallisation
- filtration
- fractional distillation
- simple distillation
- use of a solvent.

a Which method could be used to separate pure water from seawater?

....

b Give an example of a mixture that could be separated by filtration and identify the filtrate and the residue from this mixture.

Mixture:

....

Filtrate:

....

Residue:

....

c Which three methods would be used to separate a mixture of salt and sand?

....

9 Describe how crystallisation can be used to separate copper sulfate crystals from a solution of copper sulfate.

....

....

....

Challenge

10 Explain the difference between simple distillation and fractional distillation. Your answer should include examples of how they are used.

....

....

....

....

11 How could melting point and boiling point be used to test the purity of:

a water

....

b a metal

....

> ### TIP
>
> The presence of an impurity in a substance increases the difference between the melting and boiling points of the substance, making its melting point lower and its boiling point higher. The impurity also makes these temperatures less precise.

12 Brass is an alloy made from a mixture of copper and zinc. Zinc dissolves in hydrochloric acid, but copper does not. You are provided with a sample of powdered brass. Design an experiment to find how much of the brass is copper and how much is zinc.

....

....

....

....

....

....

....

....

> Chromatography

KEY WORDS

chromatogram: the result of a paper chromatography run, showing where the spots of the samples have moved to

chromatography: a technique employed for the separation of mixtures of dissolved substances, which was originally used to separate coloured dyes

R_f **value:** in chromatography, the ratio of the distance travelled by the solute to the distance travelled by the solvent front

Exercise 21.3

IN THIS EXERCISE YOU WILL:

* examine how a simple chromatogram should be set up

* practise different ways of interpreting simple chromatograms

> calculate the R_f value

> describe how to separate mixtures of soluble colourless substances.

> **TIP**
>
> Chromatography can be used to identify unknown substances by comparison with known substances and to identify pure and impure substances.

Focus

The chromatogram in Figure 21.2 compares two coloured mixtures, X and Y.

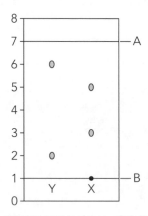

Figure 21.2: An experimental chromatogram.

13 What do the two lines A and B show?

A   ....

B   ....

14 The chromatography paper is 8 cm long. At which level was the solvent at the start of the chromatography?

....

15 Line B was drawn in pencil. Why was this?

....

16 Do substances X and Y have any components in common? Explain your answer.

....

Practice

17 Which component of mixture X is the most soluble in the solvent used? Explain your answer.

....

....

18 Both mixture X and mixture Y were made up of three components. Suggest, in each case, why only two spots are seen.

Mixture X:

....

....

Mixture Y:

....

....

19 a What method could be used to identify some of the components of the mixtures?

....

....

b How could the third component in mixture Y be identified?

....

....

Challenge

20 a Substances can be identified by measuring their R_f value. Calculate the R_f value of the component in mixture Y which moved the smallest distance. Give your answer to two decimal places.

....

....

b Chromatography can also be used to separate mixtures of substances that are not coloured. What additional step must be used to detect components of the sample in this case? Name the type of reagent involved and state how it is used.

....

....

TIP
R_f = distance travelled by substance/distance travelled by solvent

Chapter 22

Chemical analysis

> Tests for ions

KEY WORDS
flame test: testing a compound by holding a sample in a flame to discover which colour, if any, is produced
precipitation: the sudden formation of a solid when either two solutions are mixed or a gas is bubbled into a solution

Exercise 22.1

IN THIS EXERCISE YOU WILL:

- describe the colours seen in flame tests for the following metal cations: Li^+, Na^+, K^+, Ca^{2+}, Ba^{2+}, Cu^{2+}

- consider the different tests used to identify different cations and anions

- discuss how to interpret the results of these tests for ions.

Focus

1 What colours do the metal ions listed in Table 22.1 give in a flame test?

Cation (metal ion)	Colour of flame
lithium, Li^+	
sodium, Na^+	
potassium, K^+	
calcium, Ca^{2+}	
barium, Ba^{2+}	
copper(II), Cu^{2+}	

Table 22.1: Flame test colours for metal cations.

2   Carbonates are used as antacids. You are supplied with three antacids: A, B and C. One antacid contains sodium carbonate, one antacid contains calcium carbonate, and the other antacid contains both sodium carbonate and calcium carbonate.

How could you use a flame test to discover which antacid contains which carbonate(s)? Your answer should include how to perform the test and how you would interpret the results.

....

....

....

....

....

Practice

3   When a student tested the three antacids A–C using the flame test, one test gave a correct result for calcium ions, but the other two tests both gave a positive test for sodium ions. Sodium ions give a yellow colour which is so bright that it hides the colours from other ions. How could you use sodium hydroxide solution to discover which of the two antacids contained both sodium and calcium ions?

....

....

....

....

Challenge

4   Barium compounds are used to investigate problems in the digestive system. Barium compounds are toxic, so only insoluble barium compounds, which cannot dissolve and enter the bloodstream, can be used.

a   How could you test for barium ions?

....

b   Barium sulfate and barium carbonate are both insoluble in water. Why is barium sulfate always used in the digestive tract and never barium carbonate?

....

....

....

TIP

The pH of the stomach environment is around pH 1–3.

5 A group of students were given a mixture of four ions. The ions were: Ca^{2+}, CO_3^{2-}, NH_4^+ and Cl^-.

Their procedure is as follows:

A Distilled water was added to the mixture, which was stirred.

B The mixture was filtered.

C The residue was dried. Hydrochloric acid was added to it; fizzing was observed and a gas produced which turned limewater cloudy.

D The residue dissolved into the acid and a flame test was carried out on the solution. A brick-red flame was given.

E The filtrate from B was then split into two portions. The two portions were then tested separately for the ammonium ion and the chloride ion. Positive results were obtained.

a What were the two ions present in the residue?

....

b Explain how the results tell you this.

....

....

....

....

c Name the compound forming the residue.

....

d Why was it in the residue?

....

....

6 **a** The test for the ammonium ion involved heating the filtrate with sodium hydroxide. What two observations did the students obtain that confirmed that the ammonium ion was present?

....

....

....

b The test for the chloride ion involved the use of silver nitrate solution and which acid?

....

c What did the students observe that confirmed the presence of chloride ions?

....

d   Give the ionic equation for the reaction between the chloride ions and the silver nitrate solution. Your answer should include state symbols.

....

e   Name the compound present in the filtrate.

....

f   Give the balanced symbol equation for the reaction of this compound with sodium hydroxide.

....

> Interpreting analytic tests

Exercise 22.2

IN THIS EXERCISE YOU WILL:

- consider the tests used to identify different aqueous cations

- discuss how to interpret the results of these tests.

Focus

7   The tests for transition metal cations iron (Fe^{2+} and Fe^{3+}), chromium (Cr^{3+}) and copper (Cu^{2+}) involve precipitation reactions. Identify which of these cations gives the following test results.

a   Cation that gives a green precipitate soluble in excess aqueous sodium hydroxide:

....

b   Cation that gives a light blue precipitate with aqueous ammonia:

....

c   Cation that gives a green precipitate with aqueous ammonia which then turns brown on standing:

....

Practice

8   **a**   Explain why the green precipitate produced in the test in question **7c** turns brown on standing. What type of reaction is taking place?

....

....

b   Which of the ions in part **a** gives the same result with aqueous ammonia and aqueous sodium hydroxide?

....

c   Which transition metal ion in part **a** can be identified by use of a flame test?

Metal ion: ....

Result of test: ....

9   When drops of copper sulfate solution are added to aqueous ammonia, a deep blue solution is formed immediately. Explain this observation.

....

....

> **TIP**
>
> Note that the sequence of adding the copper sulfate to the ammonia solution, rather than the other way, is not the usual method of carrying out the test. Think about the difference in the observations in both cases and why they occur.

Challenge

10 A mixture of powdered crystals contains both ammonium ions (NH_4^+) and zinc ions (Zn^{2+}). The two salts contain the same anion. Table 22.2 shows the results of tests carried out by a student.

a   Complete Table 22.2 on the observations made by the student.

Test		Observations
1	A sample of the solid mixture was dissolved in distilled water. The solution was acidified with dilute HCl(aq) and a solution of $BaCl_2$ added.	A white precipitate was formed.
2	A sample of the solid was placed in a test-tube. NaOH(aq) was added and the mixture warmed. A piece of moist red litmus paper was held at the mouth of the tube.	The solid dissolved and pungent fumes were given off. The litmus paper turned ...., indicating the presence of .... ions.
3	A sample of the solid was dissolved in distilled water to give a .... solution. NaOH(aq) was added dropwise until in excess.	A .... precipitate was formed which was .... in excess alkali.
4	A further sample of the solid was dissolved in distilled water. Concentrated ammonia solution (NH_3(aq)) was added dropwise until in excess.	A .... precipitate was formed. On addition of excess alkali, the precipitate was ....

Table 22.2: Analytical tests on a mixture of substances.

b   Give the names and formulae of the two salts in the mixture.

....

....

c   Give the name and formula of the precipitate formed in tests 3 and 4.

....

....

SELF-ASSESSMENT

Tick the boxes in this table to show what you can do. Then think about how you can improve your understanding in any areas that need more work.

I can	Needs more work	Almost there	Ready to move on
understand the tests for ions			
understand why the tests are useful			
understand why more than one test is sometimes needed			

> Tests for gases

KEY WORD

limewater: a solution of calcium hydroxide in water; it is an alkali and is used in the test for carbon dioxide gas

Exercise 22.3

IN THIS EXERCISE YOU WILL:

- consider the tests used to identify common gases
- discuss how to interpret the results of some of these tests.

Focus

11 a Which gas is identified using limewater?

....

b Explain how the test is carried out.

Test:

....

Result:

....

c In the space below, give the test used and the observations for the gases oxygen and hydrogen.

i Test for oxygen: ....

Observations: ....

ii Test for hydrogen: ....

Observations: ....

Practice

12 a The tests for ammonia and chlorine both use damp litmus paper.

Describe what happens to the litmus paper in each case.

Ammonia:

....

Chlorine:

....

b Carbon dioxide and sulfur dioxide are both acidic gases. Why is litmus paper not used to test for them?

....

....

Challenge

13 a Sulfur dioxide is identified using potassium manganate(VII). Give the conditions and results for this test.

....

....

b Sulfur dioxide is acidic. What other property of sulfur dioxide does this test tell you?

....

c Sulfur dioxide is toxic and dissolves in rain to form acid rain. In what ways could acid rain harm the environment?

....

....

....

〉 Acid–base titrations

KEY WORDS

acid–base titration: a method of quantitative chemical analysis where an acid is added slowly to a base until it has been neutralised

burette: a piece of glass apparatus used for delivering a variable volume of liquid accurately

end point: the point in a titration where the indicator just changes colour showing that the reaction is complete

Exercise 22.4

IN THIS EXERCISE YOU WILL:

- consider the apparatus necessary to carry out a titration
- explain the sequence of steps performed in a successful titration
- discuss the precautions necessary to ensure the accuracy of the results.

Focus

14 Some pieces of apparatus which may be used in a titration experiment are:

- balance
- beaker
- burette
- conical flask
- measuring cylinder
- stopwatch
- volumetric pipette.

Which three pieces of apparatus would definitely be used in a titration experiment?

What is each piece of apparatus used for?

Apparatus ....

Use ....

Apparatus ....

Use ....

Apparatus ....

Use ....

15 In an acid–base titration experiment to find the concentration of ethanoic acid in a sample of vinegar, a solution of sodium hydroxide is used. Which other chemical is needed and what is its purpose?

....

Practice

16 25 cm³ of sodium hydroxide solution was measured into a flask. The vinegar solution was quickly run into the sodium hydroxide in the flask. The flask was swirled and the quantity of acid needed to neutralise the alkali was noted. The flask was then rinsed with distilled water. The titration was repeated more carefully a further three times. Readings from the burette are shown in Figure 22.1.

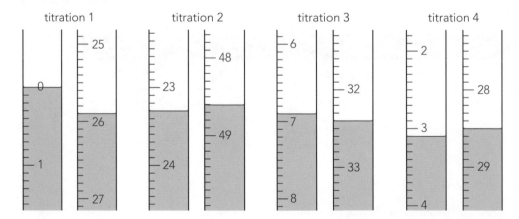

Figure 22.1: Burette readings from titration experiment.

TIP

Think carefully about which solution is being added from the burette and which solution is in the flask. This will help you understand the relationship between the volumes involved.

a   Use information from Figure 22.1 to complete Table 22.3.

	Titration			
	1	2	3	4
Final burette reading / cm³				
First burette reading / cm³				
Volume of solution A / cm³				
Best titration result (✓)				

Table 22.3: Titration results.

b   Which results in Table 22.3 should be disregarded? Explain your answer.

....

....

c   What is the mean average value obtained in the titrations?

....

d   Why was the flask swirled during the titration?

....

e   Why was the flask rinsed with distilled water after each titration?

....

Challenge

17 a   After rinsing there was some distilled water remaining in the flask. Why was it not necessary to remove this water before performing the next titration?

....

....

....

b   A second sample of vinegar, containing a greater concentration of ethanoic acid, was investigated. Would the volumes recorded in the titration be higher or lower? Explain your answer.

....

....

....

> Applying analytical tests to bottled water

Exercise 22.5

IN THIS EXERCISE YOU WILL:

- describe an application of analytical tests
- consider the usefulness of analytical tests applied to everyday situations.

Focus

The data in Table 22.4 were taken from the labels of four different bottles of spring water (A–D).

Ions present	Concentration / mg per dm³			
	Water A	Water B	Water C	Water D
calcium	85.2	85.0	36.0	4.5
magnesium	11.5	34.0	6.0	1.7
sodium	3.4	3.4	30.0	3.0
potassium	0.9	1.5	28.0	0.5
carbonate	320.0	315.0	220.0	15.0
chloride	5.6	–	15.0	5.0
nitrate	3.5	–	9.5	1.5
silicon	4.1	–	88.0	7.0
sulfate	–	85.0	4.5	4.0
total solids	270.0	396.0	320.0	33.0
pH	7.1	7.4	6.3	6.0

Table 22.4: Ionic content and pH of different samples of spring water (A–D).

18 What colour change would you see if a strip of cobalt chloride paper were dipped into water D?

....

19 What change would you see if nitric acid followed by aqueous barium nitrate solution were added to water B?

....

20 Which water is most acidic?

....

Practice

21 Which water contains most sodium chloride? Give a reason for your answer.

....

....

22 Which water would have the lowest boiling point? Give a reason for your answer.

....

....

Challenge

23 The amount of total solids is found by boiling away all the water present and weighing the solid which remains. Suggest why the value for total solids is always lower than the sum of the masses of the individual parts.

....

....

....

TIP
Will any of the ions present be affected by the heat? Think about which of the compounds you are familiar with undergo thermal decomposition.

24 Why might it be important to know which ions are present in a sample of spring water?

....

....

....

> Glossary

acid: a substance that dissolves in water, producing $H^+(aq)$ ions – a solution of an acid turns litmus red and has a pH below 7.
Acids act as proton donors

acid–base titration: a method of quantitative chemical analysis where an acid is added slowly to a base until it has been neutralised

acid rain: rain that has been made more acidic than normal by the presence of dissolved pollutants such as sulfur dioxide (SO_2) and oxides of nitrogen (nitrogen oxides, NO_x)

activation energy (E_a): the minimum energy required to start a chemical reaction – for a reaction to take place the colliding particles must possess at least this amount of energy

addition polymer: a polymer formed by an addition reaction – the monomer molecules contain a C=C double bond

addition reaction: a reaction in which a simple molecule adds across the carbon–carbon double bond of an alkene

alkali metals: elements in Group I of the Periodic Table; they are the most reactive group of metals

alkalis: soluble bases that produce $OH^-(aq)$ ions in water – a solution of an alkali turns litmus blue and has a pH above 7

alloys: mixtures of elements (usually metals) designed to have the properties useful for a particular purpose, e.g. solder (an alloy of tin and lead) has a low melting point

amino acids: naturally occurring organic compounds that possess both an amino ($-NH_2$) group and an acid ($-COOH$) group in the molecule; there are 20 naturally occurring amino acids and they are polymerised in cells to make proteins

anion: a negative ion which would be attracted to the anode in electrolysis

anode: the electrode in any type of cell at which oxidation (the loss of electrons) takes place – in electrolysis it is the positive electrode

antacids: compounds used medically to treat indigestion by neutralising excess stomach acid

atmosphere: the layer of air and water vapour surrounding the Earth

balanced chemical (symbol) equation: a summary of a chemical reaction using chemical formulae – the total number of any of the atoms involved is the same on both the reactant and product sides of the equation

base: a substance that neutralises an acid, producing a salt and water as the only products.
Bases act as proton acceptors

blast furnace: a furnace for extracting metals (particularly iron) by reduction with carbon that uses hot air blasted in at the base of the furnace to raise the temperature

boiling: the process of change from liquid to gas at the boiling point of the substance; a condition under which gas bubbles are able to form within a liquid – gas molecules escape from the body of the liquid, not just from its surface

brass: an alloy of copper and zinc; this alloy is hard

burette: a piece of glass apparatus used for delivering a variable volume of liquid accurately

carboxylic acids: a homologous series of organic compounds containing the functional group $-COOH$ ($-CO_2H$), with the general formula $C_nH_{2n+1}COOH$

catalyst: a substance that increases the rate of a chemical reaction but itself remains unchanged at the end of the reaction

catalytic converter: a device for converting polluting exhaust gases from cars into less dangerous emissions

catalytic cracking: the decomposition of long-chain alkanes into alkenes and alkanes of lower relative molecular mass; involves passing the larger alkane molecules over a catalyst heated to 500 °C

cathode: the electrode in any type of cell at which reduction (the gain of electrons) takes place; in electrolysis it is the negative electrode

cation: a positive ion which would be attracted to the cathode in electrolysis

chemical reaction (change): a change in which a new substance is formed

chromatogram: the result of a paper chromatography run, showing where the spots of the samples have moved to

chromatography: a tecŸique employed for the separation of mixtures of dissolved substances, which was originally used to separate coloured dyes

clean dry air: containing no water vapour and only the gases which are always present in the air

climate change: changes in weather patterns brought about by global warming

closed system: a system where none of the reactants or products can escape the reaction mixture or the container where the reaction is taking place

collision theory: a theory which states that a chemical reaction takes place when particles of the reactants collide with sufficient energy to initiate the reaction

complete combustion: a type of combustion reaction in which a fuel is burned in a plentiful supply of oxygen; the complete combustion of hydrocarbon fuels produces only carbon dioxide and water

compound: a substance formed by the chemical combination of two or more elements in fixed proportions

compound fertiliser: a fertiliser such as a NPK fertiliser or nitrochalk that contains more than one compound to provide elements to the soil

compound ion: an ion made up of several different atoms covalently bonded together and with an overall charge (can also be called a molecular ion; negatively charged compound ions containing oxygen can be called oxyanions)

concentration: a measure of how much solute is dissolved in a solvent to make a solution. Solutions can be dilute (with a high proportion of the solvent), or concentrated (with a high proportion of the solute).

condensation polymer: a polymer formed by a condensation reaction, e.g. nylon is produced by the condensation reaction between 1,6-diaminohexane and hexanedioic acid; this is the type of polymerisation used in biological systems to produce proteins, nucleic acids and polysaccharides

covalent bonding: chemical bonding formed by the sharing of one or more pairs of electrons between two atoms

crystallisation: the process of forming crystals from a saturated solution

dehydration: a chemical reaction in which water is removed from a compound

desulfurisation: an industrial process for removing contaminating sulfur from fossil fuels such as petrol (gasoline) or diesel

diffusion: the process by which different fluids mix as a result of the random motions of their particles

displacement reaction: a reaction in which a more reactive element displaces a less reactive element from a solution of its salt

displayed formula: a representation of the structure of a compound which shows all the atoms and bonds in the molecule

distillation: the process of boiling a liquid and then condensing the vapour produced back into a liquid: used to purify liquids and to separate liquids from solutions

ductile: a word used to describe the property that metals can be drawn out and stretched into wires

dynamic (chemical) equilibrium: two chemical reactions, one the reverse of the other, taking place at the same time, where the concentrations of the reactants and products remain constant because the rate at which the forward reaction occurs is the same as that of the reverse reaction

electrical conductor: a substance that conducts electricity but is not chemically changed in the process

electrodes: the points where the electric current enters or leaves a battery or electrolytic cell

electrolysis: the breakdown of an ionic compound, molten or in aqueous solution, by the use of electricity

electrolyte: an ionic compound that will conduct electricity when it is molten or dissolved in water; electrolytes will not conduct electricity when solid

electrolytic cell: a cell consisting of an electrolyte and two electrodes (anode and cathode) connected to an external DC power source where positive and negative ions in the electrolyte are separated and discharged

electron: a subatomic particle with negligible mass and a charge of −1; electrons are present in all atoms, located in the shells (energy levels) outside the nucleus

electronic configuration: a shorthand method of describing the arrangement of electrons within the electron shells (or energy levels) of an atom; also referred to as electronic structure

electron shells (energy levels): (of electrons) the allowed energies of electrons in atoms – electrons fill these shells (or levels) starting with the one closest to the nucleus

electroplating: the process of electrolysis in which a metal object is coated (plated) with a layer of another metal

element: a substance that cannot be further divided into simpler substances by chemical methods: all the atoms of an element contain the same number of protons

empirical formula: a formula for a compound that shows the simplest ratio of atoms present

end point: the point in a titration where the indicator just changes colour showing that the reaction is complete

endothermic change: a process or chemical reaction that takes in heat from the surroundings. ΔH for an endothermic change has a positive value

enthalpy (H): the thermal (heat) content of a system

enthalpy change (ΔH): the heat change during the course of a reaction (also known as heat of reaction); can be either exothermic (a negative value) or endothermic (a positive value)

esters: a family of organic compounds formed by esterification, characterised by strong and pleasant tastes and smells

evaporation: a process occurring at the surface of a liquid, involving the change of state from a liquid into a vapour at a temperature below the boiling point

exothermic change: a process or chemical reaction in which heat energy is produced and released to the surroundings. ΔH for an exothermic change has a negative value

fermentation: a reaction carried out using a living organism, usually a yeast or bacteria, to produce a useful chemical compound; most usually refers to the production of ethanol

fertiliser: a substance added to the soil to replace essential elements lost when crops are harvested, which enables crops to grow faster and increases the yield

filtrate: the liquid that passes through the filter paper during filtration

filtration: the separation of a solid from a liquid, using a fine filter paper which does not allow the solid to pass through

fossil fuels: fuels, such as coal, oil and natural gas, formed underground over geological periods of time from the remains of plants and animals

fractional distillation: a method of distillation using a fractionating column, used to separate liquids with different boiling points

freezing point: the temperature at which a liquid turns into a solid – it has the same value as the melting point; a pure substance has a sharp freezing point

fuel: a substance that can be used as a source of energy, usually by burning (combustion)

fuel cell: a device for continuously converting chemical energy into electrical energy using a combustion reaction; a hydrogen fuel cell uses the reaction between hydrogen and oxygen

functional group: the atom or group of atoms responsible for the characteristic reactions of a compound

galvanising: the protection of iron and steel objects by coating with a layer of zinc

giant covalent structures: a substance where large numbers of atoms are held together by covalent bonds forming a strong lattice structure

giant ionic lattice (structure): a lattice held together by the electrostatic forces of attraction between positive and negative ions

global warming: a long-term increase in the average temperature of the Earth's surface, which may be caused in part by human activities

greenhouse effect: the natural phenomenon in which thermal energy from the Sun is 'trapped' at the Earth's surface by certain gases in the atmosphere (greenhouse gases)

greenhouse gas: a gas that absorbs heat reflected from the surface of the Earth, stopping it escaping the atmosphere

groups: vertical columns of the Periodic Table containing elements with similar chemical properties; atoms of elements in the same group have the same number of electrons in their outer energy levels

half-equations: ionic equations showing the reactions at the anode (oxidation) and cathode (reduction) in an electrolytic cell

halogen displacement reactions: reactions in which a more reactive halogen displaces a less reactive halogen from a solution of its salt

halogens: elements in Group VII of the Periodic Table – generally the most reactive group of non-metals

homologous series: a family of similar compounds with similar chemical properties due to the presence of the same functional group

hydrated salts: salts whose crystals contain combined water (*water of crystallisation*) as part of the structure

hydrocarbons: organic compounds that contain carbon and hydrogen only; the alkanes and alkenes are two series of hydrocarbons

indicator: a substance which changes colour when added to acidic or alkaline solutions, e.g. litmus or thymolphthalein

insulator: a substance that does not conduct electricity

ionic equation: the simplified equation for a reaction involving ionic substances: only those ions which actually take part in the reaction are shown

isomers: compounds which have the same molecular formula but different structural arrangements of the atoms – they have different structural formulae

isotopes: atoms of the same element which have the same proton number but a different nucleon number; they have different numbers of neutrons in their nuclei; some isotopes are radioactive because their nuclei are unstable (radioisotopes)

kinetic particle theory: a theory which accounts for the bulk properties of the different states of matter in terms of the movement of particles (atoms or molecules) – the theory explains what happens during changes in physical state

limestone: a form of calcium carbonate ($CaCO_3$)

limewater: a solution of calcium hydroxide in water; it is an alkali and is used in the test for carbon dioxide gas

limiting reactant: the reactant that is not in excess

litmus: the most common indicator; turns red in acid and blue in alkali

malleable: a word used to describe the property that metals can be bent and beaten into sheets

mass concentration: the measure of the concentration of a solution in terms of the mass of the solute, in grams, dissolved per cubic decimetre of solution (g/dm^3)

melting point: the temperature at which a solid turns into a liquid – it has the same value as the freezing point; a pure substance has a sharp melting point

metallic bonding: an electrostatic force of attraction between the mobile 'sea' of electrons and the regular array of positive metal ions within a solid metal

methyl orange: an acid–base indicator that is red in acidic and yellow in alkaline solutions

mixture: two or more substances mixed together but not chemically combined - the substances can be separated by physical means

molar concentration: the measure of the concentration of a solution in terms of the number of moles of the solute dissolved per cubic decimetre of solution (mol/dm^3)

molar gas volume: 1 mole of any gas has the same volume under the same conditions of temperature and pressure ($24\,dm^3$ at r.t.p.)

mole: the measure of amount of substance in chemistry; 1 mole of a substance has a mass equal to its relative formula mass in grams – that amount of substance contains 6.02×10^{23} (the Avogadro constant) atoms, molecules or formula units depending on the substance considered

molecular formula: a formula that shows the actual number of atoms of each element present in a molecule of the compound

monomer: a small molecule, such as ethene, which can be polymerised to make a polymer

neutron: an uncharged subatomic particle present in the nuclei of atoms – a neutron has a mass of 1 relative to a proton

noble gases: elements in Group VIII – a group of stable, very unreactive gases

ore: a naturally occurring mineral from which a metal can be extracted

oxidation: there are three definitions of oxidation:
i a reaction in which oxygen is added to an element or compound
ii a reaction involving the loss of electrons from an atom, molecule or ion
iii a reaction in which the oxidation state of an element is increased

oxidation number: a number given to show whether an element has been oxidised or reduced; the oxidation state of an ion is simply the charge on the ion

particulates: very tiny solid particles produced during the combustion of fuels

percentage composition: the percentage by mass of each element in a compound

percentage purity: a measure of the purity of the product from a reaction carried out experimentally:

$$\text{percentage purity} = \frac{\text{mass of pure product}}{\text{mass of impure product}} \times 100$$

percentage yield: a measure of the actual yield of a reaction when carried out experimentally compared to the theoretical yield calculated from the equation:

$$\text{percentage yield} = \frac{\text{actual yield}}{\text{predicted yield}} \times 100$$

period: a horizontal row of the Periodic Table

periodic property: a property of the elements that shows a repeating pattern when plotted against proton number (Z)

petroleum (or **crude oil**): a fossil fuel formed underground over many millions of years by conditions of high pressure and temperature acting on the remains of dead sea creatures

pH scale: a scale running from below 0 to 14, used for expressing the acidity or alkalinity of a solution; a neutral solution has a pH of 7

photochemical reaction: a chemical reaction where the activation energy required to start the reaction is provided by light, usually of a particular wavelength, falling on the reactants

physical change: a change in the physical state of a substance or the physical nature of a situation that does not involve a change in the chemical substance(s) present

pollutants: substances, often harmful, which are added to another substance

polyamide: a polymer where the repeating units are joined together by amide (peptide) links, e.g. nylon and proteins

polyester: a polymer where the monomer units are joined together by ester links, e.g. PET

polymer: a substance consisting of very large molecules made by polymerising a large number of repeating units or monomers

polymerisation: the chemical reaction in which molecules (monomers) join together to form a long-chain polymer

precipitate: an insoluble salt formed during a precipitation reaction

precipitation: the sudden formation of a solid when either two solutions are mixed or a gas is bubbled into a solution

precipitation reaction: a reaction in which an insoluble salt is prepared from solutions of two suitable soluble salts

proteins: polymers of amino acids formed by a condensation reaction; they have a wide variety of biological functions

proton: a subatomic particle with a relative mass of 1 and a charge of +1 found in the nucleus of all atoms

proton number (or **atomic number**) (**Z**): the number of protons in the nucleus of an atom

reaction rate: a measure of how fast a reaction takes place

reactivity series of metals: an order of reactivity, giving the most reactive metal first, based on results from a range of experiments involving metals reacting with oxygen, water, dilute hydrochloric acid and metal salt solutions

redox reaction: a reaction involving both reduction and oxidation

reduction: there are three definitions of reduction:
i a reaction in which oxygen is removed from a compound
ii a reaction involving the gain of electrons by an atom, molecule or ion
iii a reaction in which the oxidation state of an element is decreased

relative atomic mass (A_r): the average mass of naturally occurring atoms of an element on a scale where the carbon-12 atom has a mass of exactly 12 units

relative formula mass (M_r): the sum of all the relative atomic masses of the atoms present in a 'formula unit' of a substance (*see also* **relative molecular mass**)

relative molecular mass (M_r): the sum of all the relative atomic masses of the atoms present in a molecule (*see also* **relative formula mass**)

residue: the solid left behind in the filter paper after filtration has taken place

reversible reaction: a chemical reaction that can go either forwards or backwards, depending on the conditions

R_f **value:** in chromatography, the ratio of the distance travelled by the solute to the distance travelled by the solvent front

r.t.p.: room temperature and pressure: the standard values are 25 °C/298 K and 101.3 kPa/1 atmosphere pressure

rusting: the corrosion of iron and steel to form rust (hydrated iron(III) oxide)

sacrificial protection: a method of rust protection involving the attachment of blocks of a metal more reactive than iron to a structure; this metal is corroded rather than the iron or steel structure

salts: ionic compounds made by the neutralisation of an acid with a base (or alkali), e.g. copper(II) sulfate and potassium nitrate

saturated hydrocarbons: hydrocarbon molecules in which all the carbon–carbon bonds are single covalent bonds

'sea' of delocalised electrons: term used for the free, mobile electrons between the positive ions in a metallic lattice

slag: a molten mixture of impurities, mainly calcium silicate, formed in the blast furnace

solubility: a measure of how much of a solute dissolves in a solvent at a particular temperature

solvent: the liquid that dissolves the solid solute to form a solution; water is the most common solvent but liquids in organic chemistry that can act as solvents are called *organic solvents*

sonorous: a word to describe a metallic substance that rings like a bell when hit with a hammer

stainless steel: an alloy of iron that resists corrosion; this steel contains a significant proportion of chromium which results in the alloy being resistant to rusting

state symbols: symbols used to show the physical state of the reactants and products in a chemical reaction: they are s (solid), l (liquid), g (gas) and aq (in solution in water)

strong acid: an acid that is completely ionised when dissolved in water – this produces the highest possible concentration of $H^+(aq)$ ions in solution, e.g. hydrochloric acid

structural formula: the structural formula of an organic molecule shows how all the groups of atoms are arranged in the structure; ethanol, CH_3CH_2OH, for example

structural isomerism: a property of compounds that have the same molecular formula but different structural formulae; the individual compounds are known as structural isomers

subatomic particles: very small particles – protons, neutrons and electrons – from which all atoms are made

substitution reaction: a reaction in which an atom (or atoms) of a molecule is (are) replaced by different atom(s), without changing the molecule's general structure

thermal conductivity: the ability to conduct heat

thymolphthalein: an acid–base indicator that is colourless in acidic solutions and blue in alkaline solutions

titration: a method of quantitative analysis using solutions: one solution is slowly added to a known volume of another solution using a burette until an end point is reached

transition metals (transition elements): elements from the central region of the Periodic Table – they are hard, strong, dense metals that form compounds that are often coloured

universal indicator: a mixture of indicators that has different colours in solutions of different pH

unsaturated hydrocarbons: hydrocarbons whose molecules contain at least one carbon–carbon double or triple bond

volumetric pipette: a pipette used to measure out a volume of solution accurately

weak acid: an acid that is only partially dissociated into ions in water – usually this produces a low concentration of $H^+(aq)$ in the solution, e.g. ethanoic acid

word equation: a summary of a chemical reaction using the chemical names of the reactants and products

The Periodic Table of Elements

Key

atomic number
atomic symbol
name
relative atomic mass

I	II	III	IV	V	VI	VII	VIII
							2 **He** helium 4
3 **Li** lithium 7	4 **Be** beryllium 9	5 **B** boron 11	6 **C** carbon 12	7 **N** nitrogen 14	8 **O** oxygen 16	9 **F** fluorine 19	10 **Ne** neon 20
11 **Na** sodium 23	12 **Mg** magnesium 24	13 **Al** aluminium 27	14 **Si** silicon 28	15 **P** phosphorus 31	16 **S** sulfur 32	17 **Cl** chlorine 35.5	18 **Ar** argon 40

Transition elements (Groups between II and III):

19 **K** potassium 39	20 **Ca** calcium 40	21 **Sc** scandium 45	22 **Ti** titanium 48	23 **V** vanadium 51	24 **Cr** chromium 52	25 **Mn** manganese 55	26 **Fe** iron 56	27 **Co** cobalt 59	28 **Ni** nickel 59	29 **Cu** copper 64	30 **Zn** zinc 65
37 **Rb** rubidium 85	38 **Sr** strontium 88	39 **Y** yttrium 89	40 **Zr** zirconium 91	41 **Nb** niobium 93	42 **Mo** molybdenum 96	43 **Tc** technetium ––	44 **Ru** ruthenium 101	45 **Rh** rhodium 103	46 **Pd** palladium 106	47 **Ag** silver 108	48 **Cd** cadmium 112
55 **Cs** caesium 133	56 **Ba** barium 137	57–71 lanthanoids	72 **Hf** hafnium 178	73 **Ta** tantalum 181	74 **W** tungsten 184	75 **Re** rhenium 186	76 **Os** osmium 190	77 **Ir** iridium 192	78 **Pt** platinum 195	79 **Au** gold 197	80 **Hg** mercury 201
87 **Fr** francium ––	88 **Ra** radium ––	89–103 actinoids	104 **Rf** rutherfordium ––	105 **Db** dubnium ––	106 **Sg** seaborgium ––	107 **Bh** bohrium ––	108 **Hs** hassium ––	109 **Mt** meitnerium ––	110 **Ds** darmstadtium ––	111 **Rg** roentgenium ––	112 **Cn** copernicium ––

Groups III–VIII continued (periods 4–7):

III	IV	V	VI	VII	VIII
31 **Ga** gallium 70	32 **Ge** germanium 73	33 **As** arsenic 75	34 **Se** selenium 79	35 **Br** bromine 80	36 **Kr** krypton 84
49 **In** indium 115	50 **Sn** tin 119	51 **Sb** antimony 122	52 **Te** tellurium 128	53 **I** iodine 127	54 **Xe** xenon 131
81 **Tl** thallium 204	82 **Pb** lead 207	83 **Bi** bismuth 209	84 **Po** polonium ––	85 **At** astatine ––	86 **Rn** radon ––
113 **Nh** nihonium ––	114 **Fl** flerovium ––	115 **Mc** moscovium ––	116 **Lv** livermorium ––	117 **Ts** tennessine ––	118 **Og** oganesson ––

1
H
hydrogen
1

lanthanoids

57 **La** lanthanum 139	58 **Ce** cerium 140	59 **Pr** praseodymium 141	60 **Nd** neodymium 144	61 **Pm** promethium ––	62 **Sm** samarium 150	63 **Eu** europium 152	64 **Gd** gadolinium 157	65 **Tb** terbium 159	66 **Dy** dysprosium 163	67 **Ho** holmium 165	68 **Er** erbium 167	69 **Tm** thulium 169	70 **Yb** ytterbium 173	71 **Lu** lutetium 175

actinoids

89 **Ac** actinium ––	90 **Th** thorium 232	91 **Pa** protactinium 231	92 **U** uranium 238	93 **Np** neptunium ––	94 **Pu** plutonium ––	95 **Am** americium ––	96 **Cm** curium ––	97 **Bk** berkelium ––	98 **Cf** californium ––	99 **Es** einsteinium ––	100 **Fm** fermium ––	101 **Md** mendelevium ––	102 **No** nobelium ––	103 **Lr** lawrencium ––

Group

The volume of one mole of any gas is 24 dm^3 at room temperature and pressure (r.t.p.).

› Acknowledgements

The authors and publishers would like to thank the following for reviewing this workbook: Farhat Deeba and Joan Hope-Jones

The authors and publishers acknowledge the following sources of copyright material and are grateful for the permissions granted. While every effort has been made, it has not always been possible to identify the sources of all the material used, or to trace all copyright holders. If any omissions are brought to our notice, we will be happy to include the appropriate acknowledgements on reprinting.

Thanks to the following for permission to reproduce images:

Cover Photo: Laguna Design/Getty Images

Andrew W.B. Leonard/Getty Images; ANDREW LAMBERT PHOTOGRAPHY/SCIENCE PHOTO LIBRARY; gougg/Getty Images; Robert Brook/Science Photo Library/Getty Images/Getty Images; Tom Grill/Getty Images; Bet_Noire/Getty Images; Hal Beral/Getty Images; Byronsdad/Getty Images; Napaporn Leadprathom/EyeEm /Getty Images; MENAHEM KAHANA/Getty Images; peepo/Getty Images; Ralph Kerpa/Getty Images; Maciej Frolow/Getty Images; oxygen/Getty Images; Peter Dazeley/Getty Images; Ray Bradshaw/Getty Images; Matthew Horwood/Getty Images; ZHMURCHAK/Shutterstock; Robert Brook/Science Photo Library/Getty Images; Hiob/Getty Images; Robert Brook/Science Photo Library/Getty Images; Anthony Brawley/Getty Images

Illustrations by Tech-Set Ltd